Take Charge and Change Your Life Today!

Trevor Bolin

iUniverse, Inc.
Bloomington

Take Charge and Change Your Life Today!

iUniverse books may be ordered through booksellers or by contacting:

iUniverse
1663 Liberty Drive
Bloomington, IN 47403
www.iuniverse.com
1-800-Authors (1-800-288-4677)

ISBN: 978-1-4620-5969-0 (sc)
ISBN: 978-1-4620-5970-6 (hc)
ISBN: 978-1-4620-5971-3 (e)

Library of Congress Control Number: 2011918291

Printed in the United States of America

iUniverse rev. date:10/21/2011

This book is dedicated to my father. He was fortunate enough to achieve great success and unfortunately had too many lessons to learn to keep it.

It's also dedicated to you, for having the courage to *Take Charge of Your Life Today!*

Acknowledgments

Thank you to those who have entered my life and shaped me to who I am today.

Thank you to my family, for enduring the years I have dedicated to this book.

Thank you to Ann Westlake, of Writer's Cramp Editing Consultants (www.wcediting.com), who let me do what I know and took care of the rest.

Contents

Contents

Introduction

A lot of great people write books about some pretty amazing topics. Professionals at the top of their fields write about teachings to guide you. Accredited dentists write about oral hygiene, and doctors write about diseases and case studies. This book focuses on the root of oneself; this is your medical journal on attitude.

I was not fortunate enough to obtain a PhD; I do not have an MD, nor do I carry any significant initials behind my name. I am certified in life simply by living, loving and learning every aspect of it.

If you had a goal to climb Mount Everest, would you ask someone who has never climbed it to tell you how? Would you read a book written by someone who has never seen it, who only studied it from the comfort of his or her home or office? I hope not. I would want someone who has not just done it once, but someone who has made it his or her passion. I would want someone who could tell me how to climb it and tell me, rock for rock, what the other side looks like from the bottom up.

This is your life manual, designed to show you how you can *Take Charge and Change Your Life Today*, from someone who has seen it from all sides.

Chapter 1

Good vs. Evil

You cannot change your destination overnight, but
you can change your direction overnight.

—Jim Rohn

People often ask me what my greatest accomplishments in life are thus far. That answer is easy: teaching people to be in charge of their own lives and, more important, every aspect of their lives today, tomorrow and beyond. I have made millions of dollars in sales and investing in real estate, owning number-one real estate companies based on what I have learned about taking charge of my own life. When I look at these things that I have done and then listen to people tell me that I have had a positive effect on their lives—how they have started to turn things around for the better, or have never felt better about themselves—the answer is just that easy. It's about you, and it's about today.

I may be only thirty-one years old, but I have only lived life for the past seven years. For the majority of my life, I got up every morning, did the same routine, went to work, sat with the same thoughts and the same attitude—and guess what I got? The same results!

The late Jim Rohn, one of the greatest personal motivators in modern history (whom I had the opportunity to meet), said it best: "You cannot change your destination overnight, but you can change your direction overnight" (*The Treasury of Quotes, 1994*). Over the years, I have tried to make my life the best I could with all that I knew. I woke every morning in the same life—my life. I knew if I kept going forward, I would achieve the life I was looking for, the life I knew I was destined for. It was seven years ago when I hit my breaking point and started to change my life.

You may be reading this because you are at *your* breaking point, or you know your breaking point is coming close. Do not be frightened; embrace it! It is going to take you from where you are today (made up of yesterday) and turn you into who you will be tomorrow. Now that's living life! Everyone *has* a breaking point. What you do with it is completely up to *you*; you will determine the outcome, based on *your* thoughts and actions.

All the people I have worked with—folks I have mentored, given sales seminars to and helped to build careers and personal lives—have made me who I am today.

Studies have been done on children who have experienced less than desirable (or even acceptable) circumstances throughout their lives and have turned out to be the bad apple. We hear this all the time: no wonder they turned out like they did, look at their parents or look at the way they were brought up, look at the circumstances in their lives. If you spent time researching my history and background, you would hear more than the term bad apple. Ask different teachers from my past, ask the people who are the closest to my heart if they thought I would turn out to be anything more than what my past pegged me for. The answer would be an obvious no. I know they were probably not far off; if I had kept going the way I was going, I would have ended up exactly that way, pegged for disaster and in a mess. I have seen people go from the top of their game to the bottom—and from the bottom to the top. The best research we can do is to learn how they went from the bottom to the top, and then we can focus on always being the best. The rest doesn't matter.

The purpose of this book is to prove that the theory about the bad apple is dead wrong! We all have a choice in life: to be better or to be just average. We have to choose to be the best and accept nothing *but* the best for ourselves and our lives—not because our parents did or did not tell us to be the best, not because we read a book or saw a TV show that told us how to make thousands of dollars a year, but because we deserve it as much today as we did yesterday.

My father used to tell me that he made the wrong choice, but that was the only choice. I love reminding him how wrong he was. There is the positive, right choice and the negative, "not so right" choice. It is not that one is bad or good. I don't live my life as bad or good; I live it by 'right' and 'not so right'.

I have made some "not so right" decisions in my life that would have taken me backward rather than forward, just as I am sure you have. I have also been fortunate enough to make the right decisions that took me to exactly where I needed to be. I do not regret the right decisions, so why regret the ones that weren't so right? I have zero regrets in my life; living with regret is like living with jealousy, fear or anger. You cannot have the life you deserve or dream of with any of those as a part of who you are.

Our oldest son reminds my mother of me as a child: he is nonstop action from sun-up to sun-down. If he can get into it, he will be into it the second we leave the room. The medicine cupboard is locked. Anything that isn't for a 3-year-old is higher than he can reach, with no possible way to climb up and help himself. For those of you who have high-spirited boys, you are in the special club and know exactly what I am talking about. When our son was wild or broke something of his mother's, my wife always told him he was being a bad boy. I, of course, put my two cents in and reminded her he is not. He is being a boy and may have made a not so right decision, and that is how he is going to learn.

I couldn't even begin to count the number of times I was told I was bad, or had an attitude problem, or was a horrible person, or was retarded. I am fortunate enough to know what the results of those words are, no matter who they came from.

I can remember being told I wasn't as smart as my sister, I wasn't as thin as my cousin, I wasn't as charming as my father. . . No, I wasn't, and you know why? I wasn't those people—*I was me!* I was absolutely 100 percent unique, and I was not going to pretend to be something or someone I wasn't.

Chapter 2

Got Goals? You Better!

A goal properly set is halfway reached.

—*Abraham Lincoln*

Right now, at the beginning of our journey, I am going to ask you to make one goal and write it down on the inside cover of this book. That one goal is that you will not be in the 90 percent of people who buy a book and never make it past the first chapter. I want you to be committed to changing your life today and joining the top 10 percent who believe they can take charge of their lives; then you *will* take charge of your life. When I first heard the above horrifying statistic, I thought it was no wonder so many books got written, published and purchased. Most people will buy a book (that's the first step in starting to feel better), and then they either put it on the book shelf or maybe read the first chapter ... and then it is gone, never to be thought about again. (Truth be known, while reading that first chapter, they may feel the happiest they have been in days, weeks or even years.)

The first step to getting on track with anything is making up your mind that you're going to do it, committing 100 percent to finishing something and setting forth. That is why it feels so good to buy a new book or borrow one. It reminds me of getting a prescription from the doctor. You know something is wrong, so you seek the help of a professional who tells you yes, you're correct, something is definitely wrong. He prescribes what will help your body get better, and you start using it. Within three days of the five-day prescription, you start feeling a lot better, so you stop taking the prescription: the problem with not finishing it until the end is that prescription is designed to complete stages throughout the term, just as life is. Those same steps are used by millions on North Americans in everything they do. Whether it is to help them fix their health, their mind or their weight, it doesn't matter. The key to finishing is not only in the starting, but in following up and following through afterward.

Each and every book I own (and there are a lot of them) has been read cover to cover numerous times. It isn't because I am running out of books to read, because I can always find more; it's that every time I read them, I find something I missed the last time.

Take the latest movie you saw at the theatre. When it was released in the local video store, 60 percent of the folks who rented were watching it for a second time. Why? Because they missed something the first time that is crucial to the story line, the climax or the ending. Reading a good book is exactly the same.

Repetition is the key to changing the way you think. It is amazing as you start to put these different, new thoughts into your conscious and subconscious mind, and they start to filter out the negative garbage you heard today at the water cooler, the junk that they used to sell newspapers with, the chewing out you got from your boss earlier. The more you fill your mind and thoughts with life-changing, positive information, the more positive your life becomes. The rest you will not even notice. You read something, see something or hear something that makes you feel good for a moment, and then you move on. Imagine, just for a second, if you felt like that *every day*! If every day of your life could be like the first time you fell in love, the first time you hit a home run, the way you felt when you held your first child, the way you felt when you closed that major deal. Imagine life through those eyes! Well, I am telling you *right now* with 100 percent certainty-it *can* and it *will*, because you *deserve* the best life.

Before you move on to the next chapter, let's get that first goal in joining the top 10 percent of people living in the free world completed. Make a note to read this book from cover to cover and tell yourself this is something you are doing for yourself. You don't have to make this next step your second goal, but if you want to climb even higher inside that 10 percent, your mission is to not only read this book cover to cover for the first time, but complete it a second time, and you will be that much closer to ensuring you have taken charge and are changing your life.

Chapter 3

Dirty Money!

Formal education will make you a living; self education will make you a fortune.

—*Jim Rohn*

I grew up in what I thought was a typical home, in a typical neighbourhood with typical parents. No, we did not have what some of the other kids in the neighbourhood had, but that only mattered when those kids were over at my house. My parents didn't get along and fought almost every time they were together. I have to give them credit, though, because they tried not to argue or fight in front of us kids. But kids can always tell what happens behind closed doors. My dad was an oil patch worker and spent the majority of his time in camps and different cities, and he was generally just not around while we were growing up. That's just the way it was and, in those times, the way it had to be. I figured we just deal with what was given to us and move on. We could complain about it and tell others how unfair it was, but that wasn't going to help us get anywhere.

Wow! Can you imagine the lives people lead and the things they have to go through, just thinking that was the hand they were dealt? Well, guess what? Life isn't a card game! Life is a series of great events full of learning experiences that we can benefit from—or be crushed under. The choice is ours and no one else's.

The people who invented a lot of the sayings we use and hear in today's world should be studied at great length and then dismissed from whatever position they hold! Phrases such as "lump it up," "money is the root of all evil," "that's just the way it is," "a fool and his money are soon parted," "money is dirty," and all the rest of those negative thoughts are unhelpful. Make a commitment to yourself that if you use those or even think of negative phrases, today is the last day you will let those words come out of your mouth, and tomorrow will be the last day they enter your mind.

A child does not have a filter for thoughts from the subconscious mind until the age of 7 or 8. Imagine what a child would believe about the world if those negative phrases are the things they hear all the time. Money is the root to all evil? It certainly is not; it is just the by-product of a job well done. Money is dirty? Explain "dirty" to me—it's not like it's the bathroom handle at the local corner store. Money is a great thing when you know what to do with it, how to treat it, when you control it and stop letting it control you ... and when you realize you have to earn it and not just make it.

One day I was trying to give advice to a friend and co-worker. It was the recession of 2008 and sales were down. He was doing a great job trying to stay positive, but I could see he was getting pretty beat up over it. He said, "You know what, Trev? I wish I would have saved some money to help me through times like these."

I said, "Aaron, I want you to write that down on something you will see every day. Do you think this will be the last time the market dips like this?" He didn't quite understand what I was getting at, so I explained it to him another way. "The market, with the huge ups and downs that we are experiencing, is a learning lesson. This down is also a learning lesson, and that's why the cycle has repeated itself continuously since the beginning of time. Experience all these great things in life and learn from them. So when times were awesome and the money was rolling in, you were spending like crazy, living an out-of-control lifestyle and not saving money. And you know what? That's okay ... this time. Now we are in a slow time, and you are struggling to make ends meet, making sacrifices you never thought you would have to make.

"And here is the clincher: it is going to be tough, but it will be all right. We are about to go through another cycle, and I can see the start of the next up period. The only thing that matters from here on out is that you learned the valuable lesson you were supposed to learn. If you do, that's fantastic, and this cycle will never affect you or your family again. If you didn't, that's unfortunate, only because the lesson is going to be even worse the second time. I have seen that cycle, and although I didn't learn everything from it the last time, I learned a lot that I put into play because I knew what I needed to do."

Now, instead of *him* having to go through it three times to learn everything, I learned the hard lesson for him. There are hard lessons and soft lessons in our world. Most people go through the hard ones, suffer through them, work their way out of them and come up more on top, in a better position than ever before. That's a fact! Most of those folks then learn that helping others to soften that hard lesson becomes a life calling.

A lot of people will disagree with me when I say one's past has absolutely nothing to do with one's future, unless one lets it. If this is the case and you disagree with me, it's all the more reason to keep reading and learning from what I am about to share with you. If my past was a road map for my life, you wouldn't be sitting here reading a motivational book written by me; you would be reading a biography about my short life, summed up by someone who did not know me, because it was too little, too late.

I believe your past can only have a positive or negative effect on your today and tomorrow *if you let it*. The difference between which affect it has is totally up to you. I chose the positive one and did whatever I could with what I had, and I used 100 percent conviction and faith to apply it every day. I applied it to everything I thought about, everything I did and everything I still do.

Don't let people tell you that they are just naturally happy. If you ever find someone who is, and the person can prove it, give him or her my phone number. It is true we are born with one gift, happiness. We watch our children at very young ages live with no fear, no stress and no worries. They ooze pure happiness, but then we get involved, as parents who have lived in today's world, and things just seem to change.

Chapter 4

Find Your "Y"

People will tell you what they think you need, they will even show you what they think you desire; but I believe your "Y" can only be found through listening.

—*Trevor Bolin*

If I had stuck to the path that was set out by my past, I would have been locked up, homeless or worse.

I meet all sorts of great people in my life, and I love to stop and ask them what their "Y" is. Once you figure out the "Y," everything else seems to fall into place. We will touch on the "Y" in more depth as we continue our journey; for now, I want you to just consider your "Y" in life. It took me a few years to figure out what my "Y" was and is and it might be the very same for you. The "Y" in a person's life is the reason for everything, it can be shaped by the past, used for the present and goal formatted for the future: at this point it doesn't matter that you know yours or not, but that you will have one.

While selling real estate full time years ago, I came across a 14-year-old named Robbie, who had been charged with trafficking narcotics. Can you imagine? Fourteen years old! At that time, he had been out of school for two years already because it was cutting into the time he could devote to his business.

There he and I were, sitting outside the courtroom while he was waiting for something. (I was there for a bank repossession hearing on a property I had listed at the time.) I asked him what he was doing sitting outside the court room in our small town. He said, "I am waiting for my dad to get done testifying. He is taking the fall for me, and that's all those dirty cops want, just someone to go to jail." This young man had let his past, his upbringing and his parents control his present—and eventually also his future.

I asked him, "If he is taking the fall for you, do you think there is maybe something to be learned from this experience?" He didn't quite get it; I don't think anyone had ever asked him that before. I said, "Did you do it?"

He looked me right square in the eye and said, "Yes, it was me, but no one will listen to me. They just want my dad because he has been selling longer."

I responded, "But you are only 14! What are you going to do if they convict your dad and send him to jail?"

"Same thing as before, when he was in jail: continue with the business and avoid Social Services until he gets out." This kid was *14*, and I had to keep reminding myself of that the entire time I sat with him. He did not sound like a typical 14-year-old boy. He looked like one, though, and I was having a tough time with that!

Hearing the certainty of conviction in his voice, you would have thought he was in his late 30s. I just couldn't believe what he had gone through already in his short life, as if it was just the hand he was dealt, and he was accepting it. I said, "Robbie, why don't you decide today that you have had enough of this—enough of breaking the law, seeing your dad in jail and living in the dark depths of society? If you had the opportunity to get back into school, graduate and become what you always wanted to be, would you? What did you want to be when you were a little boy, when you were 6? Did you dream of being a fireman or a businessman?"

He looked at me with this look in his eyes that I will never forget, and said, "I didn't want to be anything. I just wanted to be with my dad ever since my mom left, and now they are trying to take him away."

I understood the pain in his voice and, trying to help him, said, "Bobby, your dad broke the law. When people break the law, they get tried and ultimately pay the price. You know that your dad had a choice, whether right or wrong, good or bad, and he made the one he thought was right for him and right for you. I am not going to judge him because it's not my place, but he is being judged for it now."

He looked over at me again. I could tell I was starting to get to him a little, and he said, "What would you know about it? You don't know what our lives are like, with your suit and fancy shoes."

I said, "That's where you are wrong! I not only know exactly where you are coming from, but I can see the two choices you have. One is the choice I made when I was just a little bit older than you, and the other is the choice I am afraid you're going to make, which is why I am grateful to talk with you today."

Just when I felt like I was getting somewhere with him, they took him into the court room to testify. I pledged to myself that if I ever ran into him again, I would work with him to get his life turned around, no matter what it took … Unfortunately, I have not seen him since.

I truly believe that by having that 20- to 30-minute talk with him, which no one had obviously previously done, I might have opened up his mind to think a little differently, which in turn would create new actions for this young child and maybe help him find out his "Y." By being where he was at that exact time, I knew his teachers had never tried to help him find the "Y." The police figured they knew the "Y," and that was why his dad was being prosecuted. None of that is the "Y" behind the actions that were being expressed.

The "Y" stands for "why"—why we do certain things, why we make the choices that we do. As easy as that may sound, it is actually a very complex task and fits very nicely with what we are doing today. It's simple for someone to tell you to change your life, lose weight, stop drinking, control your anger. It's not as easy to find your "Y," not any easier than finding the root to those issues that come through you as negative traits, vices and the like.

Our actions are simply the result of thoughts in our minds. When we wholeheartedly believe something to be true and have a deep faith and burning desire to achieve it, our subconscious mind will help in obtaining dreams, hopes, goals and visions. That is the power of our minds. If I had the chance to figure out the "Y" behind Bobby, maybe I could have figured out what was really going on with his thoughts and his actions, and I could have helped him. One day maybe I will.

My "Y" never started as a millionaire, or with my having the ability to make a million dollars a year in sales. The thought of being successful in my small town never entered my head until I got on my path. Everything I have and have become is all because of a choice I made in life that caused ripples down my life path.

I believe we are born with a life path. How we travel down that path is the choice that we must make. We can take off ramps or on ramps, or we pull over into rest stops along the way. It's the Trans-Canada Highway of life.

When I was 14 years old, I took an off ramp because there were influences in and around my life that I let control the decisions I made. It wasn't until I was about 17 that I realized I was on a freeway to nowhere; it just kept going and going, and it certainly wasn't going to get me anywhere meaningful. I decided at that point that my "Y" in life wasn't just to be alive and be always searching for something. I knew that I had a reason for being, even if I didn't know yet what the reason was. I just knew that it wasn't where I was supposed to be.

I struggled to find the right, meaningful path for me, and I knew that my life could change. I looked back at some of my poor choices that I had made and, knowing they were not the right ones, plotted out my new life so that it would be better than what had happened so far. I considered what sorts of things I wanted to include in the journey that I was going to take. It was the most liberating feeling! I made lists of my past mistakes and why I thought I made them so that I could never make them again.

We'll get more into this in later chapters. Suffice it for now that, what appeared to be the worst things that occurred in my life actually turned out for the best!

Every decision I made in life turned out to be my 'Y." I didn't know it at the time and had to learn it the long, hard way, which is why I want you to start considering what your "Y" is, right now. Map out a course for your life by first looking into your past. Next at your present and then what you're looking forward to in the future.

These are not your goals, but your healing lessons from your past, your "Y" of today and your journey into tomorrow.

What's *your* "Y"?

Chapter 5

Look for the Signs

Men are looking for signs and miracles, but when they happen, they all look in the wrong direction.

—*Unknown*

Let's go back to where we left off. Despite a series of trials and tribulations in my life, I do not consider myself any less fortunate. If anything it is the opposite, and I find myself very fortunate for the past from which I chose to learn.

At a young age, I had a very serious weight problem that no one really seemed to notice, until it was too late. While still in elementary school, I started to pack the pounds onto a rather medium frame. It should have been easy for my parents to clue in that something was wrong.

Nowadays, when I see a young child who is as heavy as or heavier than I was (I was that big before obesity became a household word), I feel the need to not necessarily interject, but just maybe give a listening ear as to the "Y." We eat for two reasons: the ones who are naturally thin do it to live; the ones that cannot control themselves do it to deal with pain. Something you will never hear me say is "It's their fault" or "It's your fault." I don't blame anyone for anything that occurs in my life; I am responsible for the outcome. Maybe I did not cause the action, but it all lies with me. I have a choice for the outcome and choose to let it happen that way. We have to get mad enough, we have to realize we have had enough before we can say, "Enough." There has to be a breaking point in what is happening with your life, which may be why you grabbed this book off the shelf over all the others. Today you have found your breaking point and are taking charge of your life.

Many people eat in order to deal with pain. This is true for many addictions in the world today, whether it be an eating disorder, drugs or alcohol abuse. It all relates to the same thing: the pain in our mind is too great to deal with, so we mask it with something that is a little easier to handle. This will only work for so long, and throughout this book, if one of these things has been plaguing you, now is the time to realize you are going to deal with the pain and move your life forward, onward and upward.

Looking back, I can associate my weight gain to certain events in my life in which I chose to eat for comfort versus eating to live. My parents' divorce created many insecurities for me. Yes, they always fought and could barely stand to even sit at the table together, but their fighting offered a sort of comfort. People look at me strangely when I say this, especially my wife, but arguing is better than saying nothing at all. When we argue, it is because we still care enough to speak. When we are silent, it is too late, and what will come after that is the path that separates two people once in love.

We lived on a fairly tight budget, and the only non-tangible item Dad really had was a spending habit for drinking. Mom, on the other hand, liked nice things; she liked new clothes and liked to feel that after all the hard work they had put in over the years, they were doing great. I don't blame her one bit for that. If that made her feel complete at the time, or if she felt better by just having something that no one else had, that's perfect, because it doesn't last like that, without giving a little back. One of my core beliefs is you must give to get. What I mean by that is you can want or desire anything that your mind can conceive possible, but if you are not willing to give along the stages to getting it will not last. People make hundreds of thousands of dollars a year and as long as they are continually getting, without giving back they will not be able to hang onto there riches and continue to help them grow.

When I say "without giving a little back," I can think back and look at the money they earned and the mistakes they made. People now, people then let money control them as if it was the master. They were dictated by the thought of earning more, having more and spending more. They should have practiced earning more, properly saving more and learning how to control money, wealth and fortune. Now it's pretty easy to say, "Holy cow, you made some 'not so good' choices in your life." The hard part is learning from them and not making your own. Bearing in mind some people are better off apart and eventually divorced, and that was something I should have dealt with, without eating my way into more problems.

I was sexually assaulted as a child, and through the pain I suffered with that, not knowing that I could get help for what I was going through, I unconsciously decided the best way to cover it—or in my mind treat it—was to eat.

My mom had been dating a guy who was considerably older than her. After a short stint, he seemed to have the qualities she was looking for in a provider, and we all moved into his house in the country when I was 14. I can't say I blame him for being a little put out by the new living arrangements. His kids had been gone from home for so long that he had no idea what he was getting into. As a matter of fact, he had grandchildren who were older than me! Now a whole different generation was moving in under his reign.

The first week wasn't so bad. We all seemed to be adjusting as well as could be expected, and we were ready to take our first new family vacation together. It is said that you should vacation with someone before you decide to move in together, because that is a sure sign as to whether you can live together or not. I wish that option had been given to me, because the two years that followed were a true testament to a rough home life. We each have our own ideas of raising children, so who am I to say whether it was right or wrong? That's not my place. I do, however, know there was an old way, and now, thank God, there is a new way.

I am not saying it was all bad; I did learn quite a few things from our two years there. I learned how sometimes it is easier to just go with the flow rather than trying to change things or make things easier for all involved. I learned how when you throw physical abuse into the mix with emotional problems and sexual abuse, you cannot possibly eat enough to cover all three issues. Therefore I turned to something that at the time seemed like a perfect fit—drugs.

My mom always wanted to know why I had a poor attitude. I could say my emotional state was caused by the divorce, the sexual abuse, and the physical abuse. My dad wanted to know why I had a rapidly growing weight problem, and again, all three of those reasons could have been the catalyst. Eating and drugs made me feel better about myself, and my life felt normal for that brief moment.

I started to think about things that had happened in my past that were not so pleasant; then I got upset and ate to feel better about myself. When there was nothing left to eat, I started to feel bad about eating and getting heavier, and I took drugs. Talk about an endless cycle that always resulted in feeling bad!

It was years later that I learned I didn't have to feel horrible for any of this, that I did not have to eat my way into thinking I was happy or in less pain. I could develop other means in which to express my feelings to work past the issues with which I was going to have to deal.

Having been abused as a child, I found great comfort in eating, because at those moments I was at peace with myself. It felt right at the time, and it felt so good to be full. Because of this feeling of being full, I blocked out the pain I felt when I finished eating a snack (which was really the size of a full meal) only three or four hours after I had just had supper. I came to live with certain things in my life, because as long as I could feel the pleasure of being full, the pain of what was happening seemed a little less that day.

This was a prime example of coming to live with certain things in my life and the consequences they can have. My parents had been divorced for about two years, and I was eating to deal with that. Then I had to deal with being sexually assaulted. Eating felt great, being full felt great, but then I lay there and worried about being fat, about gaining even more weight, and guess what? I eventually hit over 300 pounds.

Why don't I have a weight problem today, fifteen years later? Why am I over a hundred pounds lighter? Why don't I have a drug problem as I did then? Once I learned the "Y," I learned how to associate pain and pleasure in what I do.

If we can learn from this and take the time to find the "Y" in our children, friends, family and loved ones, we can help. I don't have any problems anymore with drugs, weight or anger because I don't blame someone else for my problems.

I let go in the first book I ever read. I taught myself how to deal, heal and accept that what happened to me happened for a reason: because I would rather deal with it by eating than deal with it by fighting. I just assumed that was how my life was.

Well, guess what? If that's what I thought my life should be, or I thought it should have been something greater, either way I am right.

What's happening in your life today or what you want to happen in your life today is a matter of you standing up right now and saying, "I am going to take charge and change my life today." Say it out loud, whether you are at home reading this, on your lunch hour in the staff room or on a plane jetting between cities. You don't have to scream it or anything, or be in front of a mirror. Just say with me: "I am going to take charge and change my life today."

What a vicious cycle it becomes as we age; instead of eating because someone is mean or rude to us in school, we eat because debt collectors are calling or because we are having a hard time making ends meet. Once we decide we are going to eat to live, or eat because we enjoy it, and not because it brings us comfort, eating becomes a whole new world. You can break this cycle just as you can break any cycle. It is not easy, but the first step is telling yourself that you have the desire to do it, that you are committed and have the faith that you will succeed.

Chapter 6

Luck Has Nothing to Do with It!

It doesn't matter how many times you fail. It doesn't matter how many times you almost get it right. No one is going to know or care about your failures, and neither should you. All you have to do is learn from them and those around you because ... All that matters in business is that you got it right once. Then everyone can tell you how lucky you are.

—*Mark Cuban*

Ten percent of people are the top income earners. Is it a coincidence that the same percentage of people ever finish reading a motivational or training book cover to cover? I think not. I can look back at the past decade of my life and almost pinpoint my ups and downs in life, weight and income as to when I thought I knew enough at that time.

Jim Rohn says, "If you don't design your own life plan, chances are you will fall into someone else's plan." (*Treasury of Quotes,* 1994.) And guess what others have planned for you? Not much!

That was my problem growing up: I didn't know anything about a life plan. They don't teach this in schools. They teach you math, English, social studies and law, but they don't prepare you for the real things in life you will need, the big ticket items that will differentiate you from the bottom 90 percent.

I spent the majority of my early years in the bottom 95 percent, and that made the top 5 percent look really good. Did I think I was in the bottom 95 percent? No, of course not! But I saw what the top 5 percent had acquired and knew that that was what I wanted—I just had no idea how to get it. So I carried on my way of life, not really ever paying that much attention to it. I once heard this referred to as surviving, not succeeding. It could be viewed as the bottom 95 percent surviving and the top 5 percent succeeding.

It's time to change that a little bit right here and right now! You have committed to taking charge and changing your life today, so you are already committed to being in the top 5 percent. Surviving is for those that are unwilling to grow. You, my friend, are not only willing to grow, but you're going to do it faster and grow farther than those before you.

I was speaking to one of my good friends and coworkers one day, and I asked him if he thought I grew up with a silver spoon in my mouth, got into real estate and was just extremely lucky. People tell me that all the time! My life has nothing to do with luck, good or bad. It revolves around working hard, giving back as much as (if not more than) I get, accepting that attitude is everything and being grateful for what I have. If that sounds like too much for you to do, then I cannot help you until you want to help yourself. Start helping yourself today by committing, with absolute faith, that your life has nothing to do with bad or good luck—they don't even exist.

Chapter 7

Check Your Attitude!

The longer I live, the more I realize the impact of attitude on life. Attitude to me, is more important than facts. It is more important than the past, the education, the money, than circumstances, than failure, than successes, than what other people think or say or do. It is more important than appearance, giftedness or skill. It will make or break a company ... a church ... a home. The remarkable thing is we have a choice everyday regarding the attitude we will embrace for that day. We cannot change our past ... we cannot change the fact that people will act in a certain way. We cannot change the inevitable. The only thing we can do is play on the one string we have, and that is our attitude. I am convinced that life is 10% what happens to me and 90% how I react to it ... And so it is with you ... we are in charge of our attitudes.

—Charles R. Swindoll

As I mentioned earlier, as I grew up, my parents and teachers told me I had a bad attitude. I had a chip on my shoulder, and it caused a bad attitude. Oh, I heard them all. If we become what we are told, I should have the worst attitude in the world. But no one ever stopped to find out what caused my bad attitude.

We are not born with bad attitudes. A baby does not come into this world and think, "Oh great! Did I have to be born here, to these people in this city?" No, they are excited to be here, embarking on a new and incredible journey. That's how we should look at our lives today and tomorrow.

Every morning when you wake up, be thankful for waking up. There are a lot of people in this world that don't get to be thankful for that, but they don't realize that until it is too late. Look at the day as if it is the first day of your life, and everything is going to work, fall into place and be great. When you wake up in the morning expecting things to go wrong, what happens? They do. Throughout your day, when you expect things to go wrong or breakdown, what happens? Again, they do. I know you are reading this thinking, "Yes, true enough, but things always seem to go wrong even if I am not thinking it." For that I have one answer. That's impossible, or you wouldn't make the connection between thinking it, and something occurring.

I have trained my mind so that when I get up in the morning, I am thankful for such a great day, whether it is sunny, rainy or snowy—weather does not affect my day. If negative thoughts in the morning can change your entire day like that, think what positive ones can do!

I have tested this for years. When you think of someone you haven't heard from in a long time, you almost always get an e-mail or a call, or you bump into them in the grocery store. What you think about in your mind, you will force out of your body in results. This realization is amazing, but it has been around since before the 1930s, when we knew literally nothing about the power of the mind.

Tomorrow morning you are going to have a great day, everything is going to go your way and it will be your first day with your new thoughts. This is going to take a little practice, because negative thoughts are far stronger than positive, but stick with it and trust me when I say, "Tomorrow is going to be a great day!"

Chapter 8

Does Your Past Affect Your Goals?

Twenty years from now you will be more disappointed by the things that you did not do than by the ones you did do. So throw off the bowlines. Sail away from the safe harbour. Catch the trade winds in your sails. Explore. Dream. Discover.

—*Mark Twain*

I am often asked by my seminar attendees what in my life I regret doing or not doing. People are often shocked—or just plain don't believe me—when I tell them nothing. I do not regret anything that has happened to me in my life, or any choices I have made.

Those who live in regret live in the past. It's over and it has already happened, and the only way to change it, the only way to truly show it up, is to learn from it.

Do you think it will matter five years from now what you did this very day? Do you remember where you were and what you were doing this day five years ago? Definitely not!

I don't care what kind of scenario we are talking about. I have been in bad business deals where I have lost hundreds of thousands of dollars, as well as bad friendships where I have lost lifelong friends, yet I refuse to live in the past.

This is also your next task. Under the last sentence you wrote on the inside cover, I want you to add, "I refuse to live in the past; I live only in the present, for the future. Everything I do today for my family and for myself, whether it is financial, mental, or for my health, I do it for tomorrow."

Yesterday is too late; it is already gone. You cannot take back time; you cannot control time or bend time. You can only use the time you have been given for a day, a week or a year. Our length of time on Earth is not something we have control over ; it is up to us how we use it.

When will enough be enough for *you*? I have conquered some amazing things in my life, but I have never run across the Sahara Desert, nor have I climbed Mount Everest . I have emotionally built my body and mind to perform at its peak performance at all times. While being tested, pushed to the limits and called upon, I have ensured that success is my only option.

Every day we are tested. It is sometimes as simple as being on a diet and being offered a piece of chocolate cake, only because the person offering it feels better about eating a piece if we will. Or it is being tested by the media, the news or other negative people around us. The tests we endure everyday are what make us stronger. As much as it hurts to say no, to stand our ground because we have had enough, it may be the greatest thing we do that day.

If it were not for these tests, trials and tribulations of life, we would not grow to realize our full potential or to endure a long life, let alone 100 or more years that some people live to be, and love life as much in the hundredth year as we did in the 20th or even 50th year.

Once people realize that they are truly the owner of their own destiny, they will realize how great life is.

Life is free. We are free to choose the paths we take and get the results we ask for. None of this costs us money, so enjoy it to the fullest and never look back to reflect or try to change the past.

A few years ago, the school district in my hometown asked me to come and be a keynote speaker at a professional training day. I was extremely excited but nervous at the same time. For the first time in a long time, I was going to stand in front of the people who had something to do with shaping my life and tell them what I thought. What did I think? I have kept a fairly sheltered personal life in my hometown. Being a successful realtor at a very young age opened up my business life to anyone who listened to the gossip and rumours, but what had happened in my past stayed with me right up until that keynote session.

There I was, in front of all the teachers and support staff, including the aids, administration, reception ladies, vice principals, district employees and vice chairs. I had one goal that afternoon, making the memories of all my school years well worth it: help them all find the "Y"! I challenged everyone in that room that day to take the time to find the "Y" behind student issues. Why were some kids constantly late? Why did some of them smoke? Why did some of them have an attitude problem?

What I didn't realize at the time was that we are living in a society that does not deem it important enough to take time to find the "Y." We live in a time when the education system dictates just teaching students the same old thing they have been taught for decades, even though we tell people all the time that times have changed. This isn't the teachers' fault; they teach what they are told and taught to teach. It isn't the fault of the administrators or the school boards; this is the fault of the system.

It is the simple fact that although this new material, this new way of thinking is out there, they do not want to change from how things have always been done. I professed in front of everyone that day that many years later I knew the "Y" behind my weight as a child and the "Y" behind the reason I turned to drugs as a teenager, and once I figured out the "Y," I was able to correct the issues I had not dealt with. I hope that they can help our upcoming leaders in the future.

What happens to our dreams and goals as we get older? They get forgotten, torn apart or abandoned; they get smashed by our parents, our friends and our older siblings; they get changed by society, the economic times and by growing up. A very small number of people who knew what they wanted to be when they are 5 are actually doing that today. If we all stuck with our dreams from when we were 5, there would be so many fireman, policeman and astronauts that Tim Horton's and Starbucks would be looking at going automated.

Did I turn out to be what I wanted to be when I was 5? No, but you know what? I turned out better than I could have even imagined. How many people in one room do you think could say that with absolute certainty?

Why do you suppose people are not turning out like they see in their mind's eye? Why did you not do the things you wanted to do growing up? Because you let them get smooched, didn't update them or most of all, didn't follow them through. I am in my 30s, and I have dreams of what I want to see, who I want to meet, how much money I want to earn and many others.

The second you think you are too old to dream, you have given up. Goals are dreams for adults. If I went around telling everyone I still want to be a fireman when I grow up, they certainly wouldn't buy a book that I wrote on changing their life. However, if I told them my goal is to help hundreds of thousands of people to take charge and change their lives today, our "Y"s might come together, our thoughts produce actions and our lives start to change.

Alongside dreams, goals are the most important things we want to achieve in life. If you do not have a clear, precise plan of what you want, how do you know not only what you want, but how you are going to get there?

Just to give you an idea of how goals (dreams for grownups) look, here is a sample of mine:

The key to goals is having them written down and with you at all times. You need to be able to see your goals, feel your goals and live your goals every day of your life. You need to have daily goals, weekly goals, monthly goals and yearly goals for the rest of your life. Don't be afraid to write things down that you want to accomplish in 10, 15 or 20 years.

Life will change, and your goals can too. When I was 19, one of my long-term goals was to retire at the age of 40. Did I know I was going to be able to? Yes. Did others think I was going to be able to? No, they did not.

That was my goal. Have a look at my goals on the next page. You will see everything, from what I have planned for the next 20 years, starting from tomorrow, and how I am going to achieve it. On this page, I want you to write your goals in a similar format. Write down everything that pops into your mind over the next ten minutes. Don't think about them—just write them down. Do you want to own your own business? Have more time off to yourself and your family? Retire at the age of 40, 50 or 60? Make a million dollars (if that is one, check out www.bolininternational.com when you're done), own an island, drive a 1968 Ford Mustang Coupe with a 302 and factory air?

Whatever your goals are, they are you. Write them all down, in no particular order but in detail. Fill the page, starting now.

Your goals for this year:

-
-
-
-
-

Your goals for the future:

-
-
-
-
-

My goals for this year:

- Earn $700,000 in gross sales through real estate by helping 90 families inside my farm area achieve their real estate goals.
- Save $105,000 in my long-term savings account by putting 20 percent of all commissions away.
- Renovate the lake house by putting away $7,000 per month, and have the renovation completed by the time the snow flies and the temperature drops.
- Take a 14-day vacation with my family by completing all tasks at work early enough for an easy exit and well-deserved break.
- Finish *Take Charge and Change Your Life Today* and get it off to the publisher for release.
- Read 12 books that will help me to grow and be better than I was yesterday.
- Help a person per month (on average) to achieve their personal or business goals by working closely with them and sharing the gifts I have been fortunate enough to learn.
- Finish the restoration of my 1968 Mustang by dedicating 8 hours per week.
- Complete the seminar and training manual for *The Secret to Sales* and book 12 seminars.
- Become as great a person in this world as my kids think I am.

My goals for the future:

- Retire from sales at age 40 and focus 100 percent on helping others become the best that they can be by accumulating savings, smart investing and living within our means.
- Purchase a new Mustang Cobra in 2018 by saving $7,500 per year.
- Build our forever home in 2020 by selling our existing home and using the proceeds to live mortgage free in 2020.

Okay that wasn't so hard, was it? I will bet it felt pretty good to just dream life like that. Well, you know what? You're one step closer to achieving those goals, and it's going to feel even better when they start to happen. Goals are the first step in achieving what you desire in this world. They don't have to be difficult, and in time you will develop a more advanced system, but that was the way I started.

Thousands of speakers, mentors, coaches and trainers tell you to write your goals down and carry them with you or put them on the mirror, so you're forced to look at them every day. That's the easy way to do it. My method of goals is a little more involved but three times more rewarding.

Now that you have your goals written on the previous page, I want you to go through and number them 1, 3, 5, 10 and 20 based on how many years it will take you to obtain them. Goals that you marked with a one are what you are going to achieve in this year, starting today. For example, if one of you goal is to lose 20 pounds, that should be a 1, because it is a short-term goal that can be achieved in under a year. If you goal is to retire with $1,000,000 sitting in your savings account, that may be a 10 or a 20, depending on how committed you are to making that work. Go ahead and do this now. Come on; put your numbers beside those goals.

Writing your goals is only half the battle to achieving them. Want an inside secret that helps? Check them off as you achieve them. If one of those goals is to get a new vehicle, the day you get it, come back to the page that has your goals and check it off. Nothing feels as good as seeing a checkmark next to your goals and dreams. Trust me: cross reference back to the page, and each time you will see more checkmarks, until one day the entire page is checked off. Then you will call me to let me know how good it feels to achieve the things in life you deserve.

All right, so we have the 20-year plan. Does this mean you cannot add more to you goals? Of course not. They are *your* goals. You can modify them, add to them and shorten the timeline because you own them. These are a part of what is going to make the rest of your life the best part.

Now for the toughest assignment: I want you to take your top five 1-year goals and on a separate piece of paper write down what the goals mean to you and how you are going to achieve them. Sometimes we don't know how we will achieve it, or we don't know why we want it, but one will lead to the other.

So if you want to own an island and build a house to vacation there half of the year, and you have a 20 beside it, your write-up on this piece of paper might look like the following: "Every time I open a travel magazine or turn on my computer, and I see a picture of an island with dense green trees and white, sandy beaches all surrounded by crystal blue water, it gives me a sense of inner-peace."

That's the "Y!" (Well, it's *my* 'Y.') Yours might be similar or completely different. The "Y" doesn't matter, as long as there is one. I am going to put $1,000 away every month, or whatever I can afford, so that I am starting to save for that island. I am going to cut a picture out of my perfect island in my mind's eye and hang it in my office, in my truck and in my bedroom so that I can see that island every day. I am going to research people who have bought an island and find out how they bought it. (The Internet is an amazing resource; you can find just about anything you would ever need on it.)

The number of goals you have written down is only going to be limited by how many sheets of paper you need. I know this seems like a lot of work, but do it. This is taking charge of your life.

Now pick your top five goals from each of the categorized numbers 1, 3, 5, 10 and 20 and get to work. Write them all out on loose leaf paper. When you are done, nicely fold the sheets in half and stick them at the back of this book; we will come back to them later.

I preach about goals to everyone I meet, whether they have asked me to speak to them or have simply mentioned something that sparked a thought in my head. One day I was speaking to a colleague of mine who has been pretty successful in the sales industry. He has never really had to work at it. He didn't have written goals or anything that I take so very seriously, but he had never asked my opinion, either. We got on the topic of the slowdown in the market across the world. He had made just under $300,000 the prior year, and we were in about February and really on uncharted grounds. Then he said something that made my mouth drop: "I have redone my goals for the year in light of the market conditions."

I thought to myself, "Well, that's great; we should always update and improve our goals."

But before I could even process the thought long enough to get it out, he said, "I have changed my gross commissions earned from $300,000 down to $150,000."

I didn't know what to say! I was absolutely blown away! This was one of the first times in my career I had ever had anyone tell me he chopped his goals in half! I mean, it is one thing to be realistic and make sure you have obtainable and achievable goals, but this brought it to a whole new level of low thinking. It was negative thinking by someone who should be a truly positive thinker. This guy had been in the business for five years and made an average of at least $200,000 per year, and then this statement comes out of his mouth.

One thing I have come to believe is once you say it, it is way too late. If it is only a negative thought, it has not come into the full power of the laws of the universe; it can be undone with the power of positive suggestion (which we will get into later). But if you have said it out loud, that means you have been thinking about it a lot. I am predicting my friend will be lucky to make this newly refined goal this year. He was so scared to set a goal he would have to work hard to achieve that he took the easy way out.

Want to know what happens to people who make decisions based on the easy way out? They get out!

Chapter 9

What Are You Grateful For?

*As each day comes to us refreshed and anew, so does my gratitude
renew itself daily. The breading of the sun over the horizon
is my grateful heart dawning upon a blessed world.*

—Terri Guillemets

I have learned that gratitude is just as important as goals. The other day I was at the office and speaking to one of the folks I had been mentoring. We were in a great discussion about goals and all the different formats to use in order to accomplish them. I asked him how his gratitude weighs toward his goals. He gave me a crazy look, as if I had just asked what his pant size was. "Whatever are you talking about and why are you asking me that question?" He couldn't figure out why I would be asking him what he was grateful for. "What does that have to do with anything, Trev?"

You don't know how good you have it until you are grateful for everything you have, everything you have achieved. Be grateful for the people who have stuck close to you—and, yes, even sometimes grateful for those that haven't stuck that close. We live in a society today that has a "use them up and throw them away" attitude. It is getting tougher and tougher to be grateful for things in life when the shelf life is based on three years.

Remember your first vehicle? Heck, some of you reading this may still have that first vehicle. Remember how grateful you were when you first got it? Can you remember the feeling of freedom, as if the world was now yours, to be seen at your own speed? Do you feel that way about the vehicle currently in your driveway? Probably not, but you should.

Every morning when I get up, I have this ritual that I have been using for years. It's very simple to start, and the more you do it, the more you start to see things in a different light; everything looks a little clearer. I express how grateful I am for the things that matter to me in my life. I am thankful for my sons and my wife; I am thankful for their health and happiness. I am grateful for our home, our yard, our vehicles. I am grateful for a sunny day, for the rain and even the snow, because once we learn to be grateful for it, we can enjoy it no matter what.

Since I started doing this, I see life through a whole new set of eyes. I am grateful for my health, I am grateful for my business, our home that our children are growing up in and much more. When I was a child, I woke up every morning in the winter to look outside and see if it had snowed that night. Nothing is more exciting then waking up and seeing the world in a whole different light.

Try this tomorrow morning when you first wake up. Be grateful for the day you are given; be grateful for your husband, wife and partners in life and in business; be grateful for the vehicle you drive and the savings account you hold; be grateful for the yard that you have spent years perfecting or the yard you haven't started manicuring yet.

We have so much in our lives for which to be grateful. It doesn't matter if you live in the north, the south, in the mountains or on the water, on a golf course or next to a corner store. I am grateful everyday for my heart that beats on its own and provides the blood I need to keep me going at the rate I go; for my brain that both subconsciously and consciously works around the clock; for the ability to see the beautiful things in my life, like my wife's smile, my son's excitement, the sun shining and my ears and every other part of my body; for my rental properties and our motor home in which we spend family time; for my career and the list goes on.

Oftentimes people in my office will tell me how they are having a slow month and only doing half the deals compared to the month before. I ask them one simple question: "Were you grateful for those sales deals you did last month?" The usual answer is no.

So I ask them, "Are you grateful to be doing the amount today that you are doing?"

"Well, I sure wish I was doing more ..."

"I bet you do."

When you start your morning ritual, being grateful for what you have, for what is shared with you and so forth, you will be blessed with overwhelming instant gratification. I have done this for years and have added more items. As I am being grateful and thankful for what I have, I seem to find more things for which to be thankful.

Tomorrow morning, I want you to wake up and start your first gratuities. Start small. As you do them more often, you will build what you're grateful for. This will only work if you list them, not just being grateful for "everything."

Be grateful you are doing the amount you are doing today, and more will come. Once you're absolutely, whole-heartedly grateful for something, you see everything in a different light, the right light that will make you want to get up and take charge and change your life today.

Chapter 10

Vices ... What Are Yours?

Search others for their virtues, thy self for thy vices.

—*Benjamin Franklin*

I was asked once by a business partner if I am embarrassed to admit I had a run in with narcotics. Although it is something I don't like to admit, it was a lesson I had to endure for the future. Did I know that at the time? No, of course not. Did I learn something very valuable from that? You bet I did.

When I was 17 years old, I was still using narcotics socially. I wasn't a crack head or spending every dollar I had on them, but I was certainly doing more than I like to admit to someone I don't know.

One afternoon I realized that I had not heard from my elusive father in some time and thought I'd better check on him to see what was happening. I went over to his house, which was not too far from where I lived with my mother, and he wasn't home. I figured there was no harm in letting myself in and waiting; he had not been working lately, so he shouldn't have gone far. I walked in, and it looked like the place had been ransacked by government officials. There were bank withdrawal slips all over the table, some dated for days apart, and some only hours apart, all amounting to about a two-week period. I started to look a little closer at each slip and saw his bank account had gone from $30,000 down to $1.50 in a matter of a couple of weeks. I didn't know why at the time, but I can remember being in absolute dismay with the amount of money he had spent. We are talking more money than some people make in a year, more money than people have saved in their children's college fund—and all gone in a matter of 14 days.

I learned later that my father had started to dabble with crack cocaine. For those of you reading this who are fortunate enough to not know the effects of crack on a person, a family and society, you should include that in your gratitude speech tomorrow morning. For those of you who have had major effects in your family due to crack, heroine or other life-altering drugs, I hope I can help.

For the next seven years, I was front and centre to an unreal learning experience that I would value in the coming years. I went through a crack head's life just as if I was one, by trying to aid my father. You have to keep in mind that when I was growing up, my father was not someone I really knew; he was not around very often, and when he was, he was usually passed out from a bad drinking problem. We gave him Christmas and birthday cards, and he critiqued them and fixed our spelling mistakes with a red pen and gave them back to us. Can you remember the feeling you got when you handed in your school essay and got it back with red marks pointing out each and every mistake you made? Now imagine that being a Christmas card. We learned to keep them brief: "Merry Christmas, Dad. Love, the kids." The shorter the card, the less red marks throughout it.

First he lost his house, then his vehicle, then every possession he had worked his whole life to achieve. He lost the respect of those who knew him, including my younger sister, who for over five years did not have anything to do with him. I tried to help as any son, parent or sibling should. This was someone I had known all my life, this person who gave me life. How could I turn a blind eye? Something inside me knew I could help him, but I had to learn how. I would go home late from work each night and drive by the apartment I rented for him. If it looked like there was movement from more than one person, I would go over, bang on the door and shout "RCMP!" (Royal Canadian Mounted Police). I heard people running in all directions, climbing out the windows and running off into the alley, and it made for as much amusement as it did work. I figured that if I could intervene as much as possible with his enjoyment of it, he would start to associate doing drugs with pain and not pleasure.

When that no longer worked, I decided it was time to move him to a neighbouring city about an hour away, where his newfound "friends" wouldn't be able to make it so easy for him to be involved. It was a convenient way to keep an eye on him, and I rented him a place and did what I could at the time.

About six months later the phone rang. It was my dad, and he was in jail for trafficking marijuana to pay for his habit of crack cocaine.

"How did this happen? You couldn't have even met anyone in this short of time for you to be in a worse position then what you were when living here in the city," I scolded him. It boggled my mind! It was like using peanut butter in a trap to find a mouse; they could smell it out, and sure enough in the time morning it was inevitable. I started to think more about this situation he had gotten himself into, as well as the one I had gotten myself into. I had a choice: I could write him off like my sister did, or … You know when there is something inside of you that just won't let you make any other choice than the one your gut feeling is telling you to make? Well, that is how I made the choice to see it through.

We went through the whole court process, and the judge was fairly easy on him. At the time I was wishing he had gotten jail time, but that was for my own selfish reasons. How many drug users go to jail and dry up? Very few in today's world, so I am convinced jail would have made the situation worse. I was trying to figure out how to make it better.

We discussed a rehab program that was in the southern part of British Columbia. He was not interested in going because he believed he did not have a problem. Once I heard those words come out of his mouth, I knew the problem was worse than I had imagined. Rehab was out of the question; it would have been a waste of time and money for everyone involved.

As time rolled on, I lived my double life as a realtor and a drug councillor. The day my first son was born, the single greatest day of my life, I was in awe with everything that had happened, that our family had become three ... and then my cell phone rang. It was my father, so I answered it. His words still ring in my head today;

"I see your truck at the hospital. I am just across the street. Can I borrow some money?"

I could not believe he was now a grandfather and didn't think to ask what was happening, if everything was all right, if our new baby boy was born yet—nothing! He just wanted to get some money so he could score some drugs. I very quietly and politely told him to meet me outside, beside my truck, in five minutes. I had so much emotion going through me that I didn't know what I was going to do, but I knew it was not going to be good for anyone involved.

As I walked downstairs, my heart pumping so fast I thought I was going to go into cardiac arrest (good thing I was where I was), I couldn't hear anything but my own thoughts going a mile a minute in my head. And as I headed out the door, my intention was to walk right up to him and, as he started to talk, pop him right in the mouth and lay him out. Did I do that? No. This was my father, and that wouldn't have made things better. What do you do when you're in a drastic, desperate situation? Use desperate measures.

I took a $100 bill out of my wallet, walked up to him and, before he had the chance to say anything, said, "Don't speak." I handed him the money and proceeded. "Today, my son was born, your grandson. This is to be the happiest day of my life and the biggest accomplishment I have ever made. I know if you think back 26 years to the day I was born, before drugs became the most important thing in your life, you will feel for a second what I am feeling today. This money does not represent $100; it stands for something greater. While you take and spend this last $100, I want you to realize that you just lost your son, and you will never know your grandson."

As his eyes got glossy, he said, "Trev, don't say things like that."

I said, "Dad, listen close. I will not allow you for one second to do to my son what you have done to me for the past 15 years. I had a choice to help you, and I chose to do that. I now have to make another choice in my life that will affect my family. As long as drugs are in your life, we are not."

I turned and walked back into the hospital. I would like to say I felt great for getting that off my chest, but that wouldn't be the truth. I felt horrible. Sometimes the right things in life don't make you feel great right off the bat; sometimes they take time.

That day was the start of my dad's new life. He decided that he knew he had a problem that was affecting the only person who still cared for him—me. He knew if he didn't work on himself, how could he work on anything else in this life?

Six months later he was diagnosed with rapidly advancing prostate cancer. As I write this book, he is still with us, and he and my son, his grandson, share a relationship that I could not be happier to see. They have the kind of relationship that I wish I could have shared with my father when I was a child, but I know that that wasn't meant for me.

This life we are living is full of all sorts of lessons. Some people endure them, become stronger and go on to do great things and be great people. The rest? Unfortunately the lessons break them.

So when I am asked if I regret my bout with narcotics, I say definitely not. If I hadn't gone through that stage in my life, I would have had no way to understand the struggle my father had for 15 years, and I would certainly not have been able to help him cure his mind from an addiction that affects millions of families in North America.

I dream of a world where our children are not affected by drugs like they are today. I dream of a world where families are not torn apart and homes and lives are not lost, all due to an illegal profit.

Chapter 11

Moving On...

Letting go does not mean giving up. It means moving on. It is one of the hardest things a person can do. Starting at birth, we grasp on to anything we can get our hands on, and hold on as if we will cease to exist when we let go. We feel that letting go is giving up, quitting, and that we all know is cowardly. But as we grow older we are forced to change our way of thinking. We are forced to realize that letting go means accepting things that cannot be. It means maturing and moving on no matter how hard you have to fight yourself to do so.

—Unknown

I can relate everything I have done in my life to an experience I have had or a lesson I have learned. The ones in my future will reveal themselves to me when it is time for me to learn them.

I was so fortunate in life to learn at a young age that my parents did the best they possibly could. I have told my mom on numerous occasions, "Mom, you did a great job raising us. It was your first time, and how can anyone blame you for that? It would be like you sitting down right now and doing something you've never done—like making a painting, rebuilding a big block Chevy motor—and not expecting to learn things as you go through the process."

She learned as she went, and I can only hope that my boys learn the same things I learned with my parents. We do the best job we can with the tools we are given; we make the best decisions available with the facts we have at hand. Our best interest as parents is for our children, today, tomorrow and always. As a matter of fact, if you're sitting here right now thinking about your mom or dad or grandparents, and you have never let them know what a great job they did—not because they always made the right decision, but because they cared enough to make a decision, right or wrong in your eyes—call them or e-mail them tonight. Even if you have told them before that they did a great job, I don't think it is ever possible to be told that too many times.

The key to moving on and building the best life is forgiving those who have done you wrong, accepting that you have a choice to move on and being responsible for your life. It has taken me a very long time to forgive some of the people who have done me wrong in my life, but you know what? Once I forgave them, my life changed for the better, and things continue getting better. Their life will be tough long after mine has prospered, because they are wrestling with demons with which only they can deal.

I learned in 2002 that if I didn't forgive, I would be lugging all this baggage around with me forever. As long as I wanted to stay mad, and made the choice to do so, it would hinder me and not affect them at all. When we forgive people for the mistakes that they make, at first we don't feel like jumping up and saying, "I feel great today," but we can jump up and say, "I am on my way to feeling better today." You may be thinking, "Well, yes, but you don't know what I have been through in my life." Yes, you are certainly right, I don't, but I do know if you start to forgive, you will move on, and that is a huge step in taking charge of your life.

After all, this is your life we are talking about. Why are you letting someone else have an outcome or a say in your life, especially someone who has done you wrong? The longer you stay angry, the more pain you let yourself live in, the more it affects only one person—you!

I am not suggesting you call them up, or you go and see them and forgive them to their face, because there is a lot of pain involved in a situation like that. I am suggesting you keep a journal, writing down your thoughts and feelings, your ideas and your passions.

This is not basic psychology. Well, actually, it is that simple, so it could be. In your journal I want you to write them a letter stating what they did wrong, how it affected you, how you would have preferred they handled it and that you forgive them for it. When you write things down, you get such a clear picture of what the problem is, where the solution lies and what you can do about bringing the two together. Of all the people I have met and had the opportunity to learn from, it is those who hold something against others that continually suffer.

Jealousy is something you may have to deal with before you can move on. When I work with individuals one on one, it astounds me how jealousy can play such a major part in blocking someone's goals, dreams and visions.

The real estate industry taught me a long time ago about jealousy when I became the top producer in our area, and my inter-office friendships (I thought they were friendships) reduced by over 50 percent. If anyone in my office had come to me and asked me how I did it, so that they could use it, I would have shared it in a second. Instead they tried to trash me behind my back, avoided working with me on certain deals. And who suffered? I certainly didn't!

Chapter 12

What Have You Been Reading?

The man who does not read books has no advantage
over the man who cannot read them.

—*Mark Twain*

In Chapter 2, you committed to reading. If you can continue to read one book per month, maybe starting with this one, in a short time you will not only be thinking 100 percent positively, but you will be in the top 10 percent of people in the world. My goal is to see that top 10 percent expanded to 20 percent in this decade.

I have been committed to learning for a long time. I was fortunate to learn this secret and advance my skills to perfect it. I read a book every month. I have read some amazing books and some okay books, but I have never read a bad book. Why? Because everyone has an opinion; some may be right in my eyes, and some may be wrong, but regardless I love to learn anything and everything I can.

Cross reference back to the front inside cover, where you should have two statements written. Add this one below it: "I commit to read one book on personal improvement." Be it sales, business or whatever you are into; if you have buy it, borrow it or download it—do whatever you have to do to line up twelve books for this year. As the late Jim Rohn said, "You cannot change your destination overnight, but you can change your direction." You cannot expect one book to change your life, but it will change your life course for the better.

Here is a list of this year's books for you to seek out, buy, borrow or download. Start this process today!

1. *The Magic of Believing*, by Claude M. Bristol
2. *Think & Grow Rich*, by Napoleon Hill
3. *You Were Born Rich*, by Bob Proctor
4. *How to Win Friends & Influence People*, by Dale Carnegie
5. *As a Man Thinketh*, by James Allen
6. *Developing the Leader within You*, by John C Maxwell
7. *Maximum Achievement*, by Brian Tracy
8. *The 7 Habits of Highly Effective People*, by Stephen R. Covey
9. *The Art of Exceptional Living*, by Jim Rohn
10. *The Power of Positive Thinking*, by Norman Vincent Peale
11. *The Power of Your Subconscious Mind*, by Joseph Murphy.
12. *Take Charge & Change Your Life Today*, by Trevor Bolin. (Congratulations! You already have this book. When you finish reading it, refer it to friends and family so they can learn what you now know!)

That is your next 12 months planned out for you. I want you to commit to reading these books. Don't say to yourself you cannot afford to buy them. You cannot afford not to buy them! These are not new releases and can all be found at second-hand book stores or online—but read them, absorb them and trade them for another. If you have a few friends that are looking to get on the path to changing their lives, you can each buy a different one and trade them when you're finished soaking up the thoughts of some of the world's most brilliant people!

The very first book I ever read was *The Magic of Believing*, by Claude M. Bristol. I immediately reread it, and I have read it numerous times since then. This amazing book was written in 1948, long before the general population even knew something like this existed, and it was a phenomenal book written well before its time. *Think and Grow Rich,* by Napoleon Hill, was first published in 1937, and it is still one of the most powerful books ever written. I encourage you to read one of the original versions of the book. I found a mint condition, 1945 copy online and enjoyed it more because I could actually feel Napoleon himself writing on the paper. I took in everything he had studied and learned over twenty five years of research and just funnelling it through to me, the student.

I was at the top of my game, life was great and everything was going my way. However, I made one vital mistake: I checked my conscience at the door and brought my ego to the party. Ego is the biggest killer of friendships, partnerships, savings accounts and businesses (among a larger list of other relationships it can sabotage). I had decided that I had learned enough for what I wanted to do in life, so I quit reading, I quit writing in my journal and I didn't update or rewrite my goals periodically. I did what I call floating (which may be what you're doing right now), going off what I had learned and using that knowledge to float along in life.

When you start learning, you see the benefits immediately in your attitude, your income and your personal and business life. When you stop learning, it isn't as dramatic a change, and that's the scariest part. Most people will start to read a book or start a new seminar, see the changes and immediately assume it's working—and that they don't need to continue. What they don't see until it is far too late is when it starts to unwind and come apart.

Life gets busy, and you can have the best intentions but not always be in the right frame of mind. Well, some of the best wars are won and lost with the best intentions. So is knowledge, and knowledge is king!

It is three times easier to start than to restart. Learning is a habit, as is watching television. You cannot cut out television altogether. (Well, you can if you like, but I know that I have some favourite shows I would miss that bring a little bit of excitement to my life.) I have a habit of reading for 30 minutes every night before I go to sleep. I also read for about 15 minutes every morning when I am having "my time." I read two different books at the same time. But if you're just starting out reading, I would suggest you use the same book in the morning and in the evening. Baby steps lead to great walkers; those that run before they learn how to walk are sure to fall harder when the time comes—and it will come if the foundation is not laid right. Remember the old saying, "It's very rare one's knowledge exceeds his worth, but when it does, watch out."

When you are constantly feeding your brain, your personal life, your love life, your financial being and everything else will change! No, of course it is not as easy as just reading a book, or we would all be leading perfect lives and need no examples. But reading gives you pieces to the puzzle of your life and tells you how you can view life differently in your mind's eye. The goal of this book is to show you the pieces and have you put them together. This book is the picture on the puzzle box; I am responsible *to* you, not *for* you.

As I mentioned, you need not only to complete this book in its entirety, but to complete the small tasks I ask of you along the way. You also need to understand the teachings of it. Simply reading something is not going to be life altering; digesting it, believing it and living it will.

When I gave my son his first puzzle, he looked at the box, studied it piece by piece as he got everything into place and was so proud of himself for finally doing it. Each time he does that puzzle, he reviews the front picture on the box a little less. Now he can open the puzzle, leave the box in a completely different room and have the entire thing together within minutes because he has learned what he needed to from the first few times. You are going to read this book until you don't need to see the picture every time you change something for the better. You are going to see it in your mind's eye and start to put together your life, the life you have always wanted.

Let me start first by congratulating you. If you have made it this far into *Take Charge and Change Your Life Today*, you have already started changing your life for the better. Only 10 percent of people who purchase a book actually finish the complete book. The challenge I put out to you, is to be better than those 10 percent—be in the top 3 percent, who not only finish a book but read it for a second time in order to fully grasp the life-changing lessons. You will pick up over 30 percent more by reading it the second time, and to that is your success, your fortune and your change of life for the better.

Chapter 13

There's No Room for Negative!

*Oh, my friend, it is not what they take away from you that
counts. It is what you do with what you have left.*

—Hubert Humphrey

I am an incredibly positive person, but being positive comes with
great challenges. Negative thinkers enjoy nothing more than trying
to bring a positive person down to their level—sometimes I think
they get up in the morning and say to themselves, "I cannot wait
to find a positive thinker and ruin their day." They truly feed off of
this, whereas we positive people always feel so good about helping
someone to look at the day's little mishaps with some new light.

Negative people build their powers by affecting positive people's
outlooks on not only the day but the week, the month and even the
year, if given the chance. Those of us that are truly blessed to be
positive people need to continue to learn. Never stop learning. When
you stop learning to be positive is when the negative people come in
droves; it is almost like they have some seventh sense that tells them
when your guard is down.

Have you ever noticed it is harder to get a negative person to
think positively than it is to get a positive person to think negatively?
This happens for a reason. Our thoughts, whether they are good
or bad in nature, come out of our bodies as vibrations and cause
results all around us. This concept made me curious as to how many
people are probably thinking like this with the financial crisis that is

plaguing the world. Approximately one in six people are depressed or have had some form of major depression. So when you're at work tomorrow, look around your office. If it's not you, five of your coworkers are battling with depression. Experts predict that by the year 2020, depression will be the second biggest cause of disability. The scariest research stat of them all shows that 85 percent of people who have been treated for and recovered from depression will see a relapse. These numbers didn't shock me as much as I thought they would. Whereas doctors call it depression, I call it a loss of passion.

With that in mind, we have 15 different types of anti-depressants on the market, and yet more people becoming depressed or staying depressed more than ever before. We are born with the right to be happy, but many of us can't carry that through into adulthood. Our children and grandchildren are losing this right. We are not born with the right to be the best singer, the best mother, the best power engineer or anything else. Instead of all the pharmaceutical companies figuring out what the next, best and greatest wonder depression drug is, let's spend some money to figure out the cause.

I learned something very interesting while listening to a wonderful speaker on my favourite topic, attitude. A child does not form a conscience filter until it is between the ages of 5 and 7. That little medical fact just astounded me, and it made me want to learn more. With the subconscious mind being so receptive, it made me wonder why children turn to gangs, violence, drugs and other bad things going on in major cities. I don't think it is always parenting, but I think about Bobby (who I mentioned in the beginning of the book) and think that if he can remember all he wanted was to be with his dad when he was 5 years old, he could have allowed his conscious mind to filter for his subconscious.

What happens when we self-chatter as adults? If you are a self-chatterbox, you know exactly what I am talking about: you self-chatter about negative things happening in your life, your home and your place of work. These are not meant to be thoughts, and they are not meant to even create a change. When you start to self-chatter, do you do it when you are having your morning coffee, and you don't really put too much thought into it and go about your day? Even so, you feed your subconscious mind negative thoughts—very powerful, habit-forming, negative thoughts.

What do you think happens the next day? (You self-chatterers know exactly where I am going with this.) As you sit to have your morning coffee, your subconscious recalls the last thoughts it had and the emotions you were feeling during that time, and they come back without you even intending them to.

When I was younger I bought my wife a vehicle that was a little over our budget, but it was something she really wanted, and it fit the needs of our growing family, so I bought it.

One morning while out having a cigarette, I looked at the vehicle and I thought, "I hope we can afford this and do not lose it back to the bank, because we are overextended."

Guess what happened the next morning? If you guessed that same senseless chatter poisoned my thoughts, you are 100 percent correct. I had planted a seed of doubt in my mind when we first bought the car: that we may not be able to afford it. Weeks later, without even thinking about it, this small thought had manifested in my mind to become not only a thought but a true working and functioning worry. The next few mornings, the same thought entered my mind, but it was getting stronger and stronger. On the fifth day, I could have nearly thrown up on the driveway. It was then I had to figure out a way to fix this morning habit I had created without even intending to. I could not seem to break the thought pattern, so I had to break what was causing the thought.

Instead of going out front for my morning cigarette, I started going out back. I made it a habit that when I went out back, I would come up with a plan to pay the vehicle off. Every morning I said, "I am that much closer to having the vehicle paid off, and with every day it is paid off a little more."

Negative self-chatter can be a repetitive and destructive pattern that so many people find themselves slipping into, especially in times of economic uncertainty. They hear all the negative talk on the news, they read it in the paper and they hear it from friends. Eventually, the self-chatter burns into the subconscious. It's now getting too late because you are what you think about most of the time.

Even the most positive optimistic people can be gotten by the media. I make the choice (the positive, right choice) to not watch the news. Nothing in my day is affected by the news. It is not affected by the bad weather, nor is it affected by the stock market. Why, you ask? Because the stock market will be there tomorrow, the weather will be there tomorrow, and the news … well, unfortunately, it is there every day.

I have met some pretty interesting people in my life who watch the news, because it makes them feel better about their lives. They like to see how bad things are everywhere else, so that they realize they are not in as bad shape as they could be. That's one of the craziest things I have ever heard. You can imagine how negative these people already have to be to think that their life is not so good, and could be worse, and then they are filling their conscious and subconscious minds with even more negativity. Soon they will need to shut off the news because it is too negative and move to a third-world country so that they can see things in their world weren't so bad. They will still look good, and as we know what dangerous cycle negativity is, it will just get worse.

To those people who like to watch the news because it makes them feel better about their lives, I propose you improve your lives. Improve your thinking and improve your attitude, and you will improve your life. That is the right, positive choice that will aid you to take charge and change your life today!

Chapter 14

Quitting Time

A man is not finished when he is defeated. He is finished when he quits.

—*Richard Nixon*

Recently I have started to work one on one with people who are so pumped to change their lives but just need a little guidance to do it. I have been fortunate and learned how to do it the hard way. Most people would have quit way back like I originally tried to. Yes, you just read that last line correctly: at one point in my life, it seemed easier to quit and run than to push forward.

I had had enough of my dead-end job, my weight problems and all the negativity. If you have ever said to yourself, "I have had it, I have finally had enough, and it is time I am going to make a positive change. It is time I am going to take charge today," you are feeding your brain the information it needs to get your subconscious into overdrive and help you figure out a plan for change.

The company I had been working for declared chapter 11 bankruptcy and was taken over by a competing business. I decided to do something for me, something of which I could be proud. I became a realtor, and the course, offered through self-study in the province of British Columbia, took an average of seven months to complete before writing the final exam. I knew in my gut it was something I had to do, and do it quickly. I buckled down and completed the course material in less than one month. I was determined and had had enough with the life I was living. I worked on my course some nights until midnight and beyond. Most mornings I woke up at my table with the book over my face.

When I first started selling real estate, it was a 50/50 crap shoot as to whether I would survive. But I set myself a goal to be successful (truth be known, it was my only goal, and I didn't even really know I had set it in motion).

Have you ever have someone tell you they think you made the wrong decision, or that what you have decided to follow or pursue wasn't really for you? How did that make you feel? Well, I was told this by a few people at the time of my new career change. The problem was I was far too stubborn and had gone too far to do anything *but* follow through. What kind of person who really cares about you would say something like that, anyway? People who are jealous for not following their own dreams and goals, that's who! Why else would someone try to steer us from anything but our goals and dreams.

Take children who have dreams of being something, and their parents tell them no, they can't become that. Why not? Right out of the gate in the industry, I gave people a good reason to think I was going to do well.

The older we get, the more we get like our parents. Maybe it is because we want to protect our daughters who want to be singers but cannot hold a note or carry a tune, or our sons who want to be football players but cannot seem to catch anything other than a cold. So what? These are skills that are studied and learned, not just given.

I have never been a big sports fan, but over the course of my career in real estate, I got to meet some pretty fascinating sports legends; one I am even partners with in our offices. He played in the CFL (Canadian Football League) for the Edmonton Eskimos, the BC Lions and the Montreal Alloquettes. He won championships, rings and trophies of all sorts and followed not only a dream, but *his* dream.

I asked him once what his original dream was, and it was not to be a famous athlete. But because he enjoyed it and he worked on it day and night, year upon year, he was the best he could be at that stage. Where I am going with this is that his parents didn't tell him no, he couldn't, he wasn't fast enough, or he wasn't tall enough. However, once that seed of "you can't" is planted, whether ignored or not, it is always there, buried somewhere in the subconscious mind.

During my first two years in real estate sales, I made $75,000 gross commissions and somehow wound up $80,000 in debt from living the fast-paced life of a local socialite. I was missing mortgage payments and vehicle payments, had two of my Visas cancelled and the credit line I had seemed to rack up was on the verge of being an R9 on my credit report. I realized that although being a realtor seemed like the right thing to do, I had made a mistake.

I told my broker about the debt I was in and how I would have to go to the Alberta oil patch to work in order to try and save the last little bit I had. I thanked him profusely for everything he had done for me and wished him the best. It was there I found my first business mentor; he sat across the table from me and said, "Trev, I am not going to sit here and try to convince you to do something you do not feel is right, but I want to make you an offer that you need to consider." As I mentioned before, desperate times call for desperate measures, so I listened to the man. He continued, "If you agree to stick it out, get some training to learn the tools about the business and about life, I will lend you a few thousand dollars to get the creditors off your back long enough to get you going." I couldn't believe it: Here was a man who barely knew anything about me. He didn't know if he would even see that money again, and I can remember thinking that if he was willing to take that much of a gamble, then so was I. As I walked out of his office after thanking him, he said, "Trev, one more thing. I notice you haven't worn a suit or even a tie in over two months."

I looked down at the shirt I was wearing with blue jeans and said, "Well, today I came in to give my resignation; why would I dress up?" He just looked at me with doubt and concern on his face. But I realized he was right. For those of you that are wondering what that has to do with anything, just keep reading. You don't realize how much of an impact clothing can have on you in a sales career.

Have you ever had a day where you get up feeling kind of lazy, so you throw on some sweats or track pants? The second you put those on, you have just confirmed in your mind that you are not only *feeling* lazy, you *are* lazy. This should only be your attire for the gym, a jog, or a lazy day at home. Try getting up and feeling a little lazy and putting on a three-piece suit or an evening gown. That feeling of laziness is gone so fast that it isn't even a distant memory.

This is something that is so simple, it is actually mind blowing. We are judged by not only what we are wearing but the condition it is in. Does it have pet hair on it, is it wrinkled, are your shoes all scuffed up, are you wearing loafers with your suit when you should be wearing dress shoes? Read the book *Dress for Success,* by John T. Molloy. You will be amazed what the fashion industry knows about how to read people. That book is the first book in your second book list. After you have completed all of the books on page 62, you can start this list.

1. *Dress for Success,* by John T. Molloy
2. *The Wealthy Barber,* by David Chilton
3. *The Power of Now,* by Eckhart Tolle
4. And, of course, *anything* written by Brian Tracy

I know you are making a note of those books to get them for yourself.

The following year my income went from $75,000 gross and in debt by almost $100,000 in liquid liabilities, to earnings of $535,000. This is the same year my goal (as I was starting to learn about goals) was to make $350,000 in gross income. I could not believe what I had done. It did not happen overnight, and it not only took some time, but it took dedication. It took me to the breaking point of screaming out loud, "I have had enough—it is time I take charge and change my life, today."

Chapter 15

It's Your Weight!

*Habit is habit and not to be flung out of the window by
any man, but coaxed downstairs a step at a time.*

—*Mark Twain*

Are you at your breaking point? I have come to many breaking
points in my life—which is good, because if I hadn't, I probably
would not have gotten anything achieved.

When I was 17, I came to my first breaking point: my weight.
As discussed in chapter 7, our attitude controls everything we do.
If your attitude has become complacent, then what is controlling
your life? Negative, worthless emotions. What happens when our
lives are controlled by negative, worthless thoughts and emotions?
Nothing!

It was like I woke upon one morning and was over three hundred
pounds. I was unhappy and, even worse, I blamed everyone else for
my current sad state. I didn't stop for one second and realize that it
was me and my thinking that had put me into the situation. I didn't
realize then that the trick to lasting weight loss is to figure out what
caused the weight gain.

All the programs on late-night infomercials, and even doctor-
recommended programs from all over the world, don't offer a
permanent solution. Weight loss is nothing more than a state of
mind. Sounds easier said than done? Let me prove it.

I lost one hundred pounds in five months, and people thought I was crazy, that something was wrong with me. They always asked, "What are you taking? Is it a prescription? What happened? Did you have surgery?"

I said, "No, none of that. I finally had enough of being fat."

One day a lady asked about my weight loss, and I remember saying that I had finally had enough and decided to change my attitude, because that was what my problem was. I was living with a negative attitude and blaming everyone else for the problems I had. Heck, I was even blaming everyone else for me not being able to come up with a solution.

That day I said to myself, "Today I am taking charge of my weight and changing my life. I am taking charge of my life and changing my weight." See? Whichever way you say it, it doesn't matter, if you have the conviction behind it.

She said, without even as much as a smile on her face, "Yes. I am tired of being fat, too." That was her conviction. She was tired of being fat—no expression, no change in tone, just yes, I would like to have a million dollars in my account tomorrow.

Sure! Why not? We all would. If that is your idea of a goal, if that is your idea of conviction, then no, you are not going to get anything more than what you deserve. A good friend of mine always says you get back what you put in, and that is so true. If you cheat, you get cheated; if you lie, you get lied to; if you commit, you accomplish!.

During a municipal election in my small city, in which I was running for city council, one of my very good friends stated, "What you give to your community, you get back, and not one bit more." Have you ever heard certain things that have had such an impact, you wish they would have come from your mouth? Well, the second best is to hear them, be moved by them and start to live your life by them. My friend Lori said those words, and it was almost like a light switch flicked on.

Many years ago, I came across a quote by Brian Tracy, and after reading it I thought, "Wow," but as time wore on, I started to understand what Tracy meant. "Successful people are always looking for opportunities to help others; unsuccessful people are always asking what's in it for me" (*Building Your Network*, Brian Tracy, 2009). This is so true. and I can relate it to the way I once was. I finally realized both the knowledge I held and the experiences I had been through could be shared and would help change people's lives, starting that day.

I mentioned in the very first page that I never felt as good about anything I have done in life as I do about helping people to achieve everything they have ever wanted in life. Since then I have been fulfilled.

People tell me all the time they have a hard time making the time to try and help other people, or that they have their own problems to deal with, let alone trying to solve someone else's. I know that solving your own problems is often the hardest to figure out. But when you're busy trying to solve someone else's issues, your own problems will present themselves in a different light. Help others, help yourself!

The lady I was talking to about weight loss had no idea what her breaking point was, and she didn't have a clear goal with action objectives to completing the task. All she knew was that she wanted to be thin, but that just wasn't enough.

In my life I have learned to use my attitude to control my weight, as I have done with my knowledge. When I am not constantly learning and helping others achieve what they want, my knowledge decreases and my weight increases. Letting your attitude (the little head) control your body is the best way to get the desires you have in life. Letting your ego, your time or your emotions control them is a recipe for disaster.

I needed to lose 110 pounds over my life because of my attitude getting away from me. Yes, eating for comfort or boredom never helps, but every time life gets away from me and I allow myself to lose control of what I have going on, I gain weight. It is like my brain is saying, "Maybe he will pay attention if we slap an extra 30 or 40 pounds on him." In the meantime, there I am wondering where the heck all this weight is coming from, and I'm even scared to drink water in case that was the cause, because the weight just comes with what appears to be no reason. But there is a reason, and I know it is because I am not in control of my life.

We let outside factors control the decisions we make, and we deal with them through emotion. Is losing 110 pounds easy or fun? No, not at all. But how do you think it feels when that weight is finally gone? It is the craziest feeling ever; it is like you have your life back, you certainly have your body back, and the older we get, the tougher it gets when we need to retrain our minds as well.

So make a plan right here, right now. If you have been dealing with some unwanted, undesirable weight or any other problem that is plaguing you, you have now reached your breaking point. Decide that you are taking charge and changing your life today.

That was the first half of the plan. The second half I can help you with a bit, but you are going to have to do most of it for yourself. Find the "Y" behind the weight, or whatever the issue, and come up with a plan to fix it. Start with fifteen minutes a day; this will do a multitude of great things for you. It will give you the time to figure out the "Y," it will help you clear your head and reduce stress in your life, it will make you feel better and live longer and it will help you manage your calories. Going on a crash diet doesn't work, and taking pills may work for a while, but the weight or the problem will come back.

Until you change your attitude, you cannot change your body.

Chapter 16

Subconscious Harmony

One of the unfortunate things about our education system is that we do not teach students how to avail themselves of the subconscious capabilities.

—*Bill Lear*

In my training I try to surround myself with only positive people. As eagles soar together in the blue skies, the same is true for chickens pecking on the ground.

For example, my wife, whom I love and cherish deeply, is the type of person who would tell you she is an extremely positive person. Let me give you some examples of her positive thinking. When we first got together, as I would be on my way out the door, I said, "Good morning, Love, how was your sleep?"

Her answer 90 percent of the time was, "It was horrible! I don't feel like I even slept for an hour." Yet she has been sleeping for at least nine by that time.

I would say, "Really? I had a fantastic sleep, and I feel great this morning! Today is going to be a great day."

"A great day?" She'd say, checking the weather. "It's snowing out," or "It's raining out," or "It's going to be hot today; look at how sunny it is."

So if that is what she is like first thing in the morning, imagine what she would be like by mid-afternoon or supper. I am not going to kid you; they were some pretty brutal, early years. As I mentioned earlier, it is harder for a positive person to convince a negative person to be positive. After a few years, however, she started to see things in a different light. It has changed her life and our life together!

A lot of people think in order to have positive thinking, it must be something that one is born with, that it comes naturally. That couldn't be farther from the truth. Take my sister and me. We grew up in the same house, went to the same schools and had almost the same friends, and yet the difference between our attitudes is huge, almost like perfect strangers and complete opposites. Yet for everything else you would think we were twins (we're only 13 months apart). One evening while writing this book, I asked my little sister how positive or negative she thinks she is. She never complains or gripes or moans, and the more I think about it, she never really says anything. She just goes through life doing her thing (which is scarier than someone griping and moaning).

My sister said, "I am a very negative person—that's why I don't talk about being positive or negative." I continued to push the issue, without knowing why trying to help (whether she wanted me to or not). She said, "Here is how I have come to look at it: I am half full of negativity and half empty of positive thinking!"

I wrote it down to make sense of it so I could read it back to myself. As I was sitting there reading it, I had an epiphany and realized the only way something could be half empty is if at one time it was at least half full, if not full. Half empty of negativity—because negativity is a bottomless emotion, she is filling from the bottom. So the negativity has pushed the positive out. That's great news. All she had to decide was that she was at her breaking point; that she needed to get up every morning and start a new way to live. She needed to take charge and change her life.

The ones who gripe and moan are begging to be helped. That's their way of telling us positive people, "I want to be positive but don't know how." When I meet someone who doesn't put off a positive radiation *or* a negative one, that's when I worry. They are so complacent with being nothing all the time that I know the problems are far deeper than just being negative or positive.

Living in harmony is something everyone strives for in life, whether they know it or not (and whether they admit it or not).

When your life is not in harmony, whether it's your thoughts, your actions, your attitude or your emotions, you won't be able to achieve anything you desire. It all starts by admitting your true desires and putting them in writing. You then need to figure out what is your burning desire; write that down beside your newfound goal. From that point, ask yourself, "Does it fit in harmoniously?"

A lot of people are striving for something, yet it does not come. Why? Because what they are after, what they are trying to achieve, does not fit in harmoniously with their lives. Some children are told that money is the root to all evil. I have seen it on pastors' walls, and I have heard people say it and believe it. Money *isn't* the root to evil; not knowing that money is just a servant is the root to all evil. When you hear something and believe it, and you build it into your subconscious mind, then without the right reprogramming, it is impossible to live in harmony!

How are you ever going to earn lots of money, be wealthy and prosperous or become a millionaire, if you have been programmed to believe living in harmony means living without? It's time to reprogram!

Tonight before bed, I want you to tell yourself what it is you need to reprogram your subconscious mind to achieve so that you can get what you desire. For example, if you're in sales and keep telling yourself throughout the day that sales are slow, sale are slipping, the market has slowed and you're lucky to do half the sales you used to, you're feeding your mind junk. You need to feed your mind good, nutritious information: that this slow down has given you a chance to reinvent your business and do better than ever; that it has given you the opportunity (and yes, it *is* an opportunity) to focus, restructure and get back to the basics of why you love doing what you do.

Every day I tell myself that I am wealthy, I am prosperous, and money is good and is my servant. Throughout different times of the day, I tell myself that deals flow to me in abundance because I treat my clients like family to ensure they get the best service that I can give. By knowing that deals flow to me in abundance, and by knowing that in exchange of getting, I give, I don't even question whether or not this will come to me—I know it will, and I am telling you it will for you, too! This is part of living in harmony. When you live your life in harmony, everything seems to fall into place. I know that sounds too easy to be true, but it isn't. Let me explain even further.

If your subconscious mind believes something, and you are trying to live with something that doesn't add up to what your core belief is, you're not living in harmony. When you do not live in harmony, you will never find wealth, happiness, peace or anything else you so desire in life. If you work with people to earn a living but have said that you do not like people, this is exactly what I am talking about.

I knew a realtor once that told me he didn't like people. One day he shared with me that his sales had slipped by more than 50 percent in a busy market. He could not figure out why; he was doing the same marketing, and he hadn't changed his beliefs in customer service, so why was this happening to him? I asked him what kind of thoughts he had been thinking lately. He looked at me sort of funny and didn't know if that was something he should tell me. As he started mumbling over different thoughts he had been having over the past few months, the one comment that grabbed my attention was that he was tired of working with people. Instead of stopping him in his tracks, I let him finish the rest of his thoughts and asked him which one he thought could be affecting his business. Because he did not have an in-depth knowledge of how powerful negative thoughts could be, he had no idea what he was doing wrong.

I would say 95 percent of the general public, whether in sales, customer service, stocking shelves or pumping gas, has no idea of how powerful both the positive side of life (and unfortunately, the negative side of life) can be.

When I explained to him that his comments toward disliking people was sabotaging his career, he couldn't believe something so small and insignificant would have that much of an effect, that quick. Once I explained to him how this worked with living in harmony, it was like a switch suddenly turned on, and he said, "So what now?" I told him not to stress out about it. First, realize what the problem is; second, discover what is causing it; and third, decide how to repair it. Once we worked together to repair what had been done, and he changed the way he thought about working with people, his whole life changed for the better.

You cannot tell yourself that you don't like something, when your subconscious mind knows you earn an income from doing the opposite of what you're telling it. It is a quick downward spiral from that point. Be true to yourself, always—you deserve it!

It is like people who check their bank accounts every day expecting to see a negative account balance; when they see a negative balance, they say, "I can never save any money." My favourite is folks who buy lottery tickets or enter draws, yet at the same time they state that they never win anything and don't know why they even play or try. Just think what could happen if someone entered a draw with an absolute belief they *would* win—not that they *could*, or they *hoped* they would, but that they *would* and that they deserved to!

Chapter 17

The Power of Suggestion

To begin with, you must realize that any idea accepted by the brain is automatically transformed into an action of some sort. It may take seconds or minutes or longer – but ideas always produce a reaction of some sort.

—Scott Reed

I use the power of positive suggestion for everything in my life. I don't mean getting up in the morning, looking in the mirror and saying, "You are great today! You look great today! Are you getting a little thinner, or maybe a little thicker on top of that head of hair?" No, nothing crazy.

I talk in the present tense and never the future. I am not hoping to be happy 10 years from now, so why would I wish for happiness in the future? A wish is just a hope, dream or goal without the knowledge of how to make it happen. I don't wish to be happy; I am happy right now, right here, today. I don't wish to have money fill my pockets; money is filling my pockets right now, right here, today.

As a man thinketh, so he is. You are what you think about and do, most of the time. You will become what you worry about all of the time. A negative emotion or negative thought takes time, because we think of negativity in the future sense.

If you spend the majority of your time worried that your car is going to get repossessed, that you cannot afford it, that you will never amount to living with anything more than pay cheque at a time ... guess what? You're right. You're not right because *I* want you to be; you're right because *you* want to be.

What if, instead of saying that you are in debt and you're drowning, you say that you have some bills to catch up on, but you are floating your way to the top. You are not going to lose your vehicle or your house; you are going to come up with a plan to have them paid off within the next two years, three years or five years.

When you start to change the way you think about the life you are currently living, things start to look a little sunnier and appear a little clearer.

Ever notice how when you start a savings account that comes directly out of your account, like attracts like? I bought a retirement savings plan once, although I could have cared less about saving at that age; it just felt like the right thing to do. Well, like attracts like, and within a few years it went from $15,000 to $100,000 not from big deposits or huge withdrawals, but by simply coming up with a plan for deposits when and for how much I could afford. Then I let the rest work in my favour. As we attract what we think about, so does everything else in the world.

How many times do you drive around the block waiting for a parking space, all the while saying in your head or out loud, "It is noon, there are going to be no parking spots available," or "It is supper rush and I am late. I am never going to find a space to park." Or what about when you're on your way to the grocery store, to work in the morning or to a late show, and you are running late and hit every single red light along the way?

Something has to be said for the power of suggestion. I have ridden with people who, when in a hurry, will actually say at the first red light, "Oh great, I will probably hit every red light!" Next time you're in a bit of a rush, picture all green lights at every intersection. It isn't enough to ask for it; you have to picture it. I use this all the time. Some call it luck, some call it coincidence; I call it positive energy and thinking. Then when I do get one red light out of four or five green in a row, I am being stopped by something even more powerful than my mind, and I need to be aware of that.

Let me give you the most out-of-this-world example of the power of suggestion. When I was still learning how attitude controlled what I did, I actually let my mind conceive the notion that my family would be better off with my insurance money than my life. I can't believe now that I ever thought that! If you just read that line and then said to yourself, "Whew, I am glad someone else has had that thought," get on your computer, go onto my website www. bolininternational.com and send me an e-mail, because we need to chat! You see, I hadn't reached my breaking point yet. I was coasting with no plan, and when you coast with no plan, you usually fall into someone else's. This is your life, and you need to live it like you dreamed it.

This is the craziest thought that anyone can have, but the great news is it might be your breaking point to the situation you are worried about—not eating, not sleeping, overeating, hot flashes, erratic decisions or negative thinking. This is about the most negative thought you could allow to enter your mind. That was when I knew the problem that was plaguing me had to be dealt with right then. All the money in the world means nothing compared to the ability to be here and change the world one person at a time.

The next day, I woke up, made sure I said my gratitudes and then wrote down one goal for the day, and that was to deal with the problem at hand right away—not later. I dealt with the problem, and I did do it that day. Why? Something that seemed too complex to even try to work out a solution for suddenly appeared in a different light.

Different people are going to tell you what they think of a situation or another person, or even maybe you, and they have that right. But no one has the right to judge you. *You* have to right to be happy, to be the best that you can be; you have the right to live your dreams no matter what they may be. Embrace your rights and learn how to live with the power of positive suggestion. Don't be so hard on yourself.

Chapter 18

That's Affirmative!

*Knowledge is two-fold, and consists not only in an affirmation
of what is true, but in the negation of that which is false.*

—*Charles Caleb Colton*

Daily positive affirmations are an absolute favourite of mine. I enjoy getting them, but even more, I enjoy sharing them.

How many of you start your morning and say, "Argh, it's Monday," or, "Oh, I have so much to do today," and then you proceed to grumble around getting ready for your day? Then you get to work; check the local news; read the paper; check out websites, bulletins, stock market sites; and basically set you up for a bad day no matter what else happens in your day. A lot of people do that every day of their lives; they just don't know how to do it any other way. And worse yet, they don't know the impact their regular routine has on them.

Well, guess what? There is a better way, a way that will change the way you feel about your day, your week and your life. Here is my typical daily routine. I am not saying you have to do things just this way to make it a great day, but you can start with *one* thing, and it will guaranteed be a better day.

Get up one hour earlier in the morning. As soon as you open your eyes, do your gratuities. Say them out loud and think of as many things as you have to be grateful for. (Don't be too loud, though. if you wake your partner, that could make it a bad day no matter what!)

When those are done, pull on some track pants, shorts or jogging pants (something great for walking in); grab your iPod, mp3 player or Walkman; pop in your favourite album of Bob Proctor, Brian Tracy, Jim Rohn or numerous others; and take the dog (or go alone) for a 20- to 30-minute walk to get your metabolism pumping, to get your creative juices flowing and to wake you up to a beautiful day. Some might say it's -20 degrees out, or it is raining. That's even better. You get to witness Nature at her best; you get the opportunity to prepare for your day, and all this just makes it that much greater.

When you are finished with your walk, get ready for work and think about your daily goals—what are you going to accomplish today, what sort of things you want to add to your list, what you want to get involved in. Have your coffee and your breakfast (which is the fuel for your mind getting through the day). On the ride into work, don't you dare turn on the radio, the news or anything else that could negatively affect your day.

There, see? You're taking charge and changing the rest of your life by changing today. I guarantee this will change your day and break the cycle. Change your routine, because it feels great.

When you get into work, remind yourself that you are fortunate to have a job or career, that you even get paid to provide the service you do.

When you get to your desk or work station, check your e-mail. And when you have signed up at www.bolininternational.com for a daily affirmation, read it and study it, and then do a great thing: forward it on to someone or a group of people whom you know will benefit by having as great a day as you.

Write down a list of one, three or five things you are going to accomplish today. Whether it be personal or business, put it on the list. Don't make the list too hard for your first few days; start off simple with things that you have been putting off doing, and tackle them. As you work through the list, check off each item upon its completion. Nothing feels as good as checking off a daily goal and knowing that you set out to do it—and not only did it, but did it today.

Do not waste time around the water cooler discussing the bad stock market, the dropping housing prices or anything else that can bring you down. You are relative to the five people you spend the most time with during the day. If you hang around with three negative people and two positive people, chances are you will be negative. If you can surround yourself with positive, like-minded people, guess what? Like attracts like. Stop letting people affect you. You are bright, talented and free to be as happy as you want.

On the drive home, you are not going to turn the radio on just because it's easy. You're going to continue to listen to the speaker you started this morning. Every time you're in the car, you are in attitude school and are changing your life for the better, one commute at a time.

Tonight when the kids are in bed, or when your evening events are done, instead of plopping down on the couch in front of the TV, continue reading this book for the first or second time, or pick up another motivational book. (If you have finished one, refer again to my reading list.) Spend at least 30 minutes a night reading something that is going to improve your business, your life, your relationships or your well-being. By reading 5 nights a week for 30 minutes and listening to your CD or mp3 on your commute in and out of work, within a year you will have positive thinking and a life-altering attitude. With this you will change your life, and it all started the day you bought this book, committed to reading it cover to cover and started living your life, the best life and the life you deserve.

Chapter 19

Pay Yourself First!

The amount of money you have has got nothing to do with what you earn ... people earning a million dollars a year can have no money, and people earning $35.000 a year can be quite well off. It's not what you earn, it's what you spend.

—Paul Clitheroe

Right now you have a 5 percent chance of becoming a self-made millionaire. I know, this sounds a little crazy, but statistics have shown that 1 in 20 people will become a millionaire in their lifetime.

If becoming a millionaire in your lifetime is on your list that you wrote earlier, good for you! That was one of my early goals as well. The question is, what can you do today to start on the path to ensuring you are in the 5 percent that make it to millionaire status?

Pay yourself first. If you are in a commission paid job, when you receive your cheque, take 10–15 percent of that and stash it away in an account that you will not touch. Set it up on Internet banking that your deposit gets made for you. This sounds difficult, but trust me, it is not. After four to six months, you will have created the habit, and nothing will feel more normal.

If you are working for a corporation, it's sometimes even easier because they can and will do it for you. You can set it up that your chosen percent is taken off and held back for you by the company in an account set up by them. At the end of the year they can pay you out this amount. Your taxes will have already been paid for you, and you get a handsome chunk of cash that you can put into a savings account of your own once a year *that you do not touch.*

People are not saving enough money anymore. Until 2008, we have had such good economic times worldwide for so long that people forgot what it was to have a rainy day, let alone a rainy year. Good times come and go, and they come again. People forget, have other wants and put them before their needs. This is a need.

If you make $60,000 a year and put away 15 percent, that leaves you with 85 percent of your net income for living expenses. If you invest this saved money every year and you are 30 years old right now, with retirement in 35 years at a conservative amount of interest, you are looking at accumulating $1,146,987 in a savings account for your retirement!

So you turn the great age of sixty-five. Then what? Even by continuing to live off this money for the next 10 years, the interest alone will pay you over $60,000 per year, without even dipping into the original savings. Can you imagine retiring at sixty-five, continuing to earn over $60,000 a year and being able to have your original investment earning interest continually for years to come? Now *that's* a great feeling!

I used relatively safe numbers, safe amounts and safe calculations just to give you an idea of how easy it is to become that 5 percent that will make it to millionaire status in a lifetime, and I think 65 is hardly a lifetime. I hear that's when the fun really starts!

I would like nothing more than for you to take this program and make it fit to your lifestyle, and it will because all you have to do is provide the goal. I have provided the incentive for you, and the rest, the interest, just falls into place.

More and more programs are being offered to encourage savings. You don't have to be a millionaire to become a millionaire. You just have to think like one and do things they do; like attracts like.

Sometimes the worst thing people can do when markets get tight and stocks or mutuals show signs of weakness is pull out. I had clients and friends pull over $200,000 from the bank because of a decrease in stocks, bonds and mutual funds. I quizzed them about what they had done with the money when they pulled out, and guess where it was? In the closet or in a safe. Guess what it is doing in the closet? Nothing!

Once I kept $25,000 in a safe that we had in our old house. I had always planned that this money would be there in case we needed it. This sounds great in theory, but truth be known, it holds zero value until it is put back into circulation. This money could have made me more money, but the second I cashed it out and it held no value, it attracted no value.

When markets fluctuate, the best thing you can do is buy more at a lower price, and it will average off your first purchase.

I spoke to many financial experts between 2005 and 2008, which were very different years. The key learning tips they had in common was don't touch the money; leave it there over the long haul. When you pull large amounts of money out of an account and put it in the safe at home, the mattress at home, or in the wall, it is useless. Money only has value when it is being traded and is growing.

Human nature is a curious thing. When real estate prices started going down, all you heard was how people lost large amounts of money. I quizzed them as to what they bought and sold the property for, and the answer was very often the same: "Oh, well, we didn't sell."

I gave them a puzzled look and asked as politely as possible, "Well then, how did you lose so much money if it was never really yours in the first place?" This is a perfect example of how you can look at things the right way or the not so right way.

If you didn't actually have the money in your hand, it was never yours. Real estate prices go up and down; the cycle has been the same for years, and it will continue.

If you purchased your home in 2003 for $232,000, and the market peaked in 2006 for $310,000, and now it is 2009 and down to $209,000, you never gained or lost anything, because in 2012 you may sell and it might be worth $356,000. As long as you are not selling in tough real estate markets, there is no such thing as a bad market. More fortunes are made in bad times than in good times.

Don't get me wrong; there are corrective, soft and unstable markets, but that doesn't make them bad. It makes them full of opportunity for those who have positioned themselves properly.

One of the wealthiest developers in Canada was asked what his secret was to earning millions of dollars and becoming one of the richest men in the country. His secret was simple: seize the opportunities that markets such as this present. When markets are crazy busy, we think they will never end. We earn money and spend it and live for the times. People buy and sell real estate, buy and sell stocks—but they don't save! Then in slow times, they don't have the extra money to invest. They slow down buying real estate or stocks and just focus on selling (which the opposite of what they should be doing).

We see these cycles every so often, and it doesn't change. So why are people not learning? These cycles will continue to be a major part of our world until we change.

Learn from the latest economic downturn. Realize this market will change and will go back up. Start saving as we discussed in the plan and be ready for the change. When the market picks up and times get crazy busy again, continue saving, building and working on getting into that 5 percent that will be a millionaire. Don't follow the pattern of most people who, when things get busy, forget their plans and goals and start living for the day.

I always tell friends and families that when they really want to get ahead, save everything possible through good times, living like a scrooge while others are spending like crazy. They may look at me strangely, and they don't always get it at first, but they will.

I had clients who were looking to build a home, and my advice to them was to sell the existing home when the market was high, rent something cheap until the market started to drop and *then* buy land and build.

When the market shifts, everything shifts with it, and timing is the key to the process. Lumber costs are down during a recession, trades are cheaper, concrete is cheaper and wages are considerably lower and more competitive. It is a win-win situation, but you have to be prepared. I know this isn't for everyone, and most are not even close to being prepared, but there are signs to watch out for without being too timid to not want to live.

Do you know the actual meaning behind the word recession? It is the reduction of a country's gross domestic profit for at least two quarters. If the past shows us it is a reduction of GDP for two quarters, then we know it is the media that drives it longer than that.

What do you think would happen if the media quit reporting on the recession, and people were able to believe and stick with the positive thoughts they choose to have? I am not saying we should live in a sheltered cave or be too afraid to turn on the news or radio, but just think about the possibilities.

A few years ago, Al Gore became a major frontrunner for the effects of global warming. Everyone got scared because reports came out that it was progressing worse than expected, and we were warned to change our lifestyles. At my home, it is often around -42 degrees Celsius, and within two days it can be +9 degrees. I have lived in Northern British Columbia my entire life, and when winter starts in October and ends in May, I can relate to a global cooling.

I am not getting into all of this because I want to try and give you an insight into global warming or cooling; I am giving you an insight into how media works its negativity into our homes, our lives and our families. Fear sells more papers than anything else. When people are scared of global warming, gangs, recession or falling real estate prices, they pay attention. They stop thinking the way they should think, and they start to self-chatter about what is happening to others.

You cannot take thoughts out of your subconscious mind once they are inside. The only way to start to beat down the negative thoughts that are pulling your life down is to get back to more positive thoughts, more positive affirmations, to be able to shrink and minimize the room the negative ones are taking up.

I normally don't go on about how the effects of positive and negative to such a detail, but this is one of the more important ones you must work into your life schedule so that together we can take charge and change your life today!

Chapter 20

It's a Long Way to Fall

Success is falling nine times and getting up ten.

— *Jon Bon Jovi*

I have built up fortunes and happiness only to stop paying attention and stop learning every day. I let my life run on as most people allow their lives to just run on, and I found myself back in the very same spot worrying about money, life and bills, and generally walking around with a smile on my face that was only skin deep.

I was startled with how fast things quickly withered and deteriorated. It seemed as if it was only months before things took a turn for the worst. Although it took more than a year for my life to hit bottom, now that I look back, it was noticeable every month—what was happening, how my thoughts were changing. My outlook on life had become corrupted by the negative media around me and by the doom and gloom of life.

I had spent what I saved because I did not have a plan for any savings; I burned through my company account because more was going out than was going in at that stage of the game. I had learned one true secret, and that was how to earn money, but I had not learned how to manage it or keep it. I surely didn't learn that I was the master and money was my servant.

So many people in the world think that they will make money if they work the eight-to-five job with a one-hour lunch break and two fifteen-minute coffee breaks and dozens of conversations around the water coolers.

I have been fortunate enough to witness some amazing things in my life that have lead me to believe, with absolute faith, that it does not matter what you do to earn money. You will never be able to make money; the Canadian Mint makes money, but people have to earn money, and they can do it two ways. The first, which would be what I described earlier in this paragraph, is wasting work time because you have not realized how disliking your job has a direct influence on disliking your life. Or, you can come to the realization that once you do something you truly enjoy, something that gives you a reason to want to get out of bed in the morning and go for 4 hours, 8 hours or 15 hours, you are going to something you will love. Once you find something you absolutely love to do, you will never again work a day in your life.

I started selling real estate 12 years ago; I had finally found something I loved to do with every fibre of my body. I had always enjoyed my previous jobs, but once I started helping people achieve their dreams in home ownership, I realized I only liked parts and pieces of what I had done before I did this.

I talked about real estate constantly and dreamed about it, and believe it or not, I even talked about it in my sleep. This was how I knew I truly loved it: I have not taken one sick day in over a decade. I took some time off when my sons were born and for unfortunate tragedies in life, but never once did I not want to go to fulfill what I longed to do. I refuse to fall victim to a cold or the flu, and I'm for sure not going to let them affect me and my life.

What is the best part about loving to help others? The by-product of this is earning a very good living. When you love what you do, and you do it with all your heart while being grateful for it, you will become financially wealthy.

When you see all the greatest scams on the news about how rich people in our society scam and steal and then lose it all, or go to jail or even worse die, it is because they are not living in harmony with what they are doing to earn the wealth. If you don't truly believe you are worth earning $100,000 or $250,000 a year, you never will earn it until you change the way you think.

A coworker and I were having a candid discussion one day about the ability to earn half a million dollars in a single year. He had earned $300,000 in the previous year, and I had earned just fewer than $200,000 in commissions. He said to me, "Trev, why don't you go after it?"

I said, "Oh, my gosh, that would be impossible to do."

"I don't think it would; you should do it," he said.

I left his office thinking to myself, "He is right, that wouldn't be impossible. Well, it would if I didn't want to, or felt I didn't deserve it, but I do." I changed my goal right then and there, from $250,000 in earned commissions up to $535,000.

Changing the goal was step one. Step two was the addition of what I needed to change in order to achieve this new goal. Upon coming up with the solution of what needed to change, the three basics were in place for this new goal.

1. I had the goal.
2. I had the right mindset to perform this task.
3. I had put the necessary sales systems into place.

I decided that in order to do this, I needed to help satisfy other people's needs first, and the by-product would take care of itself. I had to assist 200 families make a move and do a great job for them, and it was time to start.

On December 20 the final numbers were in, and I had earned over $500,000 in commission in a single year. This had been unheard of in our area, and boy did it feel good to show myself that it could be done! It was then I realized if I could earn half a million, I could use it to earn a $1,000,000 in a single year.

It is also possible to do more than one thing that you love to do. I do it every day. Sometimes we get paid monetarily for it, and sometimes it is just knowing we have helped change a life; by doing these things you truly get a sense of how great your life is. I am not suggesting you call tomorrow and quit your current job because you truly are unhappy with it. I would put a plan into motion and write down what it is you would truly like to do, something that makes you smile whenever you think about it.

Now remember you are going to be working to earn your fortune, so saying something like being a queen or a movie star doesn't really work overnight.

Writing it down plants the seed in your mind of what it would look like if you were doing what you love each and every day. Put a picture in your mind and then memorize what that picture looks like. You need to reference that picture every day. As you start to see it, you will piece together how to get what it is you desire. This is your mind working to achieve everything you desire. Expand your plan as more and more information comes to you, but you have to believe in it and work with it with absolute faith.

You must be cautious and not obsess about it or not really believe you can do it. Follow the easy steps to allow your mind to put it out there, and watch for things to start to change a little bit. Opportunities will start to present themselves, but you have to know what they look like.

You will find the steps to get to what you want and what it is; you see start to be laid out in a plan in your mind's eye. Every day you will get a little bit closer.

Let me give you a different example so you know how serious I am. Take this plan I used and implement it with the discussion we just had.

I decided I wanted to open an office or buy my existing office. I am sure this is something a lot of realtors decide because it seems like the next logical step in a career. I tried the approach that everything is for sale, and I should just buy one! Well, that works for the foolish, because although everything may be for sale, if it isn't the price you had in mind, that is a pretty clear indication it is not going to work for your benefit.

I added to my goals sheet "Own my own real estate office by the time I am 30 years old." I pictured this and thought of this day in and day out. I was not consumed by it, however I was aware of its existence in my mind's eye. Steps started to be laid out for me to achieve this desire. The first step was the realization of the mind's eye. The next step was to design a flyer for a town to see how much interest there was for me to move one of my team members down and work there through our office. The response was huge. That lead me to think, "Instead of just moving a team member down, I should open an office."

I requested the paperwork from RE/MAX International and got to work on what it would take. In the meantime, they called my existing broker-owner and told him what I was looking into doing. He then approached me about the three of us opening an office in that area. It took about a year and a half to bring the idea to fruition, and there were many steps, but they all started with the first step, the mind's eye. We made a great partnership (we will touch on partnerships a little later). This wasn't luck or a fluke that it happened. It was knowing exactly what I wanted, being open to the ideas of how to get it and letting my mind play the key controller to fulfilling my desires.

Partnerships can be wonderful things, or they can be the biggest disaster in life. I have had numerous partnerships; some worked okay, some absolutely flourished and some I try not to even think about. Forming a partnership in business is very difficult, let alone forming one what will work well for a long time.

The worst thing that can enter a partnership is greed and/or ego. Once these enter, whether it's a partnership of two, three or even four doesn't matter. It will ruin the partnership, and everyone will lose money, faith, friendship and more.

Sometimes getting out of a partnership is a lot harder than getting in, but it is generally well worth it. A partnership needs to consist of like-minded people who each bring their own strengths to the table. If it consists of two or three people who have the same strengths, it will not work. But if each of the parties brings something the other is not good at, doesn't enjoy doing or just really doesn't want to do, it will work great! Before entering into *any* partnership in life, make sure all partners are on the same page with what each will work toward and what each will add, do and take away.

My partners in the real estate companies each bring their own experiences, knowledge and attributes, as do I, and it works like clockwork. We sometimes disagree, and we each want something different at times, but that's why it works the best at the end of the day. We have the same goals and can work on our own and together to make them happen.

Chapter 21

Have a Little Faith!

Keeping your dreams alive. Understanding to achieve anything requires faith and belief in yourself, vision, hard work, determination, and dedication. Remember all things are possible for those who believe.

—*Gail Devers*

Throughout the book you have read about faith, and to each his own. My faith may be very different than yours, and yours may be different from your children's, your parents' and your neighbours. Our faith is what sets us apart from any other species. I am not referring to going to church or praying before a meal or before bed, although that's great too. I mean the faith that we have and hold as humans.

I have a faith inside me that knows there is something more out there than just the world happening as it does. When people say that's just the way of the world, I always think, "If only it were that easy."

I had the good fortune to meet Bob Proctor. Bob is one of the forefathers of getting inside the mind, figuring out how it works and using it to achieve everything one desires. I attended one of his Life Success training seminars, and we had an opportunity to speak together at length.

He told me of a time when he was conducting a seminar, speaking on faith and God. One of the people from the audience mentioned how good the seminar was until "all this God stuff got brought up." Bob told me he went over and handed the man a tulip.

When the man asked what that was for, Bob replied, "I am going to finish up the conversation I was having. If you can make me another one of those in the meantime, I will come back and get them both from you." The gentleman in the audience was stunned and didn't know what to think. When Bob returned he said, "I see you still only have one."

The gentlemen replied, "I cannot make one of these."

Bob said, "No, I know you cannot, but someone did!" I will remember that story forever, and every time I see a beautiful flower, I often think about it and am reminded that someone somewhere made that single flower for us to enjoy and be grateful for. Who made it is completely up to you, but the power of knowing someone made it is called faith.

I have also had the good fortune of learning about a lot of different religions and seeing how faith works for different people. Religion is one of the oldest and still most controversial topics of our time. Nothing shocks me as much as those who do not believe at all. Again, there is nothing wrong with having no religion if you so choose, but having no *faith* will give you stumbling block after stumbling block throughout life. Without faith, we as humans would rank even closer to the apes. Have you checked your faith lately?

I mentioned doing gratuities in the morning, which is a form of faith. I have mentioned being able to hold something in your mind's eye and putting out the thoughts and actions needed to create it for you; that's faith. Each and every thing we desire to create will be created through the knowledge needed to perform such a deed and through the unquestioned belief that faith is a part of something bigger than all of us.

The next time you are challenged with something—when the answers to your questions seem so hard that you think you might never be able to find a solution, or things are so bad that life seems to be throwing you all of these curve balls—I want you to use your faith knowing an answer is out there, your intuition to be able to receive that answer to your question and your burning desire to better guide you through the question, the answer and the change.

I have used these three priceless tools for the majority of my adult life.

We are given these tools but are never shown how to use them. Once we learn what they are, how useful they can be and how they can change your life, we have gone farther and done more than most men and women. What did people like Albert Einstein have that you do not? What about some of the great teachers and philosophers of our time? They had knowledge of how their minds work and how to achieve the great things in life they desired.

People who long to be wealthy and plunk money in slot machines, or who play the lottery faithfully every week, are never going to be wealthy. Being wealthy isn't winning a million dollars. If you ask anyone who never had a million dollars until they won it or inherited it, most will tell you they are broke or close to it.

Being wealthy is in mind, body and spirit, not in bank account. To truly be wealthy, you have to learn what it takes to be just that, what it takes to stay that way and what it takes to live with that. You have to get rid of the mindset that money is evil and that you don't deserve to have money or the things that come with having a lot of money. You have to understand that you do not make money, you earn it, and you have to provide something to earn that money. People who rob banks are not wealthy; drug dealers are not wealthy; no one who does something illegally or hurts another for gain is wealthy.

You need to combine a lot of little yet extremely important things, like faith, into your life. You need to believe that what you're going to achieve is there and ready for you; you have just not done yet what is required for it to find you.

I have always believed that what we have in store for us is whatever our imaginations can conceive and our minds can attract. Do you honestly believe that good things are in store for only some people? Not a chance. Do good things happen to bad people? Yes. Do bad things happen to good people? Of course. Both sides of the paradigm are within this universe; the difference will only be what your mind manifests for itself. I cannot stress enough that if you wait for bad things to happen to you, or if you talk about them coming, they will … it's just that simple!

Here is my favourite line: "Well, bad things always happen in threes, and this is only two." Who made that up? I would like to find out what happened to him, to coin a phrase like that. Bad things don't always happen in threes; you notice there isn't a saying on the right side of that, like "Good things happen in fours, so boy, are we lucky!"

Tough times will come, and they will come more than once. I believe they come the first time to teach you the difference between good and bad times. They come the second time to ensure that you learned the last time, and if not, it will be a painful lesson all over again. I believe they are only bad if you allow them to be and let them take over the positive, creative side of your thinking.

Everything in this great world is here for our use and for us to benefit from. Whether this be the riches of the worlds or the lessons of the times, only you get to decide what is in store for you, and when!

Life is a fine balance, and you must have inner balance in order to find the things you want in life. I was having a conversation with a friend of mine one afternoon, and he relayed to me what a hard time he was having making ends meet. I asked him what sort of things he had been doing or thinking about when it came to this. As he was talking, I made notes on everything that was causing him to not be in harmony. He said in one sentence the sum of the entire problem: he was scared to go to his mail and see nothing but bills and invoices, and he would open the box up, and sure enough there were nothing but bills and invoices. However because he was looking from the inside, he couldn't see what he was doing wrong.

Then in the next sentence, he told me that he was doing what I had told him to do and was thinking about positive things, like earning money. I asked him if he was earning money, and he said yes, and he was quite happy about it. I asked him if he was earning money and doing everything that he felt was right, where was the money going? He said, "That's simple, it's going to all the bills and invoices that come in the mail."

All I said after that was, "Interesting!"

He then used the power inside of him and said, "That's it, I am expecting money to come in through work, which it is, but I am also expecting it to go out due to work, so in my mind when I see money coming in, I also picture it going right back out again. Life is giving me what I see in my mind, what I am basically asking for."

Sometimes without even knowing, we sabotage ourselves unintentionally, whether it is our income, our families or our lives. We are all born with the right to be happy; the rest is up to us and determined through our thinking. Everything must be balanced in your life for it to be the best life you could work toward. None of us make it through childhood, teenage years and adulthood with just the right life. We all have experiences that shape who we are going to be today and tomorrow, and faith can help us get there.

Some years ago, a dear friend of mine was having some pretty difficult experiences with her marriage. She tried not to let anyone know what was happening, but it is tough to deal with alone. I noticed, over the course of time, that her attitude and work ethic had started to change a little for the worse, and before she knew it, she was in an utter, complete mess personally and financially. The worst part was she knew exactly what was causing the mess and felt helpless against doing anything to improve it. She confided that she knew that her marriage was having a negative impact on every other aspect of her life. I asked her what she thought she should do about it, and I told her not to answer me with, "Oh, don't worry, it will sort itself out." The problem with letting it sort itself out is that she would not be in control of the result, which was not good.

She told me she knew what she had to do; she just didn't want to have to do it. I painted her a picture of what it would look like 2, 5 or 10 years down the road if this carried on, and it was not a very pleasant picture for her or anyone else involved.

Within a couple weeks, she had decided it was time to get her life sorted out and back to being in charge of her life. She divorced the man she had been married to for 10 years, got her mind wrapped around putting back together what she had lost, and away she went.

This process lasted for a couple years, but it was one of the best life lessons she will ever go through, and she came out on top. She is remarried today to one of the nicest guys I have had to opportunity to meet, and he worships her to no end. Once she realized it was as bad as it was, what she really wanted in her life for her to be happy was out there, she just had to go after it, and did she ever! She had faith in herself, and you should, too!

Chapter 22

What Did You Do?

Money is usually attracted, not pursued.

—*Jim Rohn*

Earning money is a by-product of providing a useful service or product to another; we covered this theory a couple chapters ago. If you do it right, and your product or service is of use and welcomed by others, you will receive the by-product, which is earning remuneration (being paid). If your product or service is not useful, or it harms others, you will not be rewarded this remuneration.

Look at the great businesses of our time. First they offer something, and then they are rewarded through payment for what they offer. The Keg Steak House offers the most tantalizing steak on the market. They then provide you with what they promised, which is great food, good atmosphere and top-notch service. Then they get rewarded for what they offered you. This is a very general idea of what I am referring to, but I think you get the picture. If you went there and the food was horrible, the atmosphere was smoky and dark, and the service was dreadful, would you pay them? Would they expect to get paid? Of course not! One must follow the other.

Your work is the exact same thing: if you provide your 100 percent good service, you will be rewarded for it. If you provide 75 percent of what a customer expects, you will be rewarded based on that as well. If you provide 50 percent, you'd better hope the company is not looking at scaling down ... and if you provide 25 percent, I can imagine your boss has a meeting planned with you for next week.

People often say to me, "I only get an hourly wage, so I get paid the same whether I put in 50, 75 or 100 percent." Each time I hear this, I cannot help but share how much I don't agree with them. You are being rewarded through remuneration based on the quality of work you give. You will get exactly what you have coming to you. Ever heard that old saying? It works for the positive more than the negative. I have seen people go from being janitors to senior management, from being assistants to running their own company, the low man on the totem pole becoming a CEO.

Does this happen overnight? Of course not, but it will happen once you realize that you get back what you put in and not a smidgen more.

During my sales career, if I did not want to do 100 percent, I would not get rewarded 100 percent. I would get back exactly what I offered and followed up on.

Two parasites of life are greed and ego. When any decision—whether it is personal, business or family orientated—is based on greed or ego, you do not get rewarded at all. We have all seen great leaders fall; excellent businessmen go out of business and spouses separate when greed and ego came into play. They are both very negative features that go against living in harmony.

Ego should not be confused with confidence or with knowing what one wants or deserves. Likewise, greed should not be confused with the hunger to earn or going after what one feels he deserves.

I spent one year letting greed and ego run my business. No sound decisions can be made, nor can a rational thought be produced, as long as greed and ego are in control of our thinking. They cloud judgement, they cost companies and people thousands if not hundreds of thousands of dollars and they will ruin any partnership because the greed and ego started running the show.

Ego is the "I" or self of a person; a person as thinking, feeling, and willing, and distinguishing itself from the selves of others and from objects of its thought (Dictionary.com). Does this sound like something that will bring you a benefit by helping others?

Let's look at the true meaning of greed. It is the excessive or rapacious desire, especially for wealth or possessions (Dictionary. com). If you have a partner in business or in life, that could be coming down with either of those parasites, have a discussion sooner rather than later. Trust me, there is not enough room for either one of those behaviours in the relationship or partnership, let alone all three of you.

A partnership can be an exciting and rewarding adventure. As with your life partner, a business partner offers insight to the real need and the pure emotions to becoming the best together. Nothing feels better than being on the top of your game, your field or your life than to share it with someone who put the same amount of blood, sweat and tears in as you have. You can build great businesses and great relationships with the right partners. The key has always been bringing something of equal value to the table and sharing it with those you are working with in order to achieve a similar goal.

Chapter 23

Average or Normal?

*Good leadership consists of showing average people
how to do the work of superior people.*

—*John D. Rockefeller*

While researching for this book, I wanted to find out how many
people could become the best they could be, could become what
they deserved to be. I uncovered some amazing facts. In the United
States 2008 census, there are a whopping 112,386,298 households
with 12,437,500 household in Canada (2006 Canadian Census).
That number is not nearly as amazing as the next one: there are
54,057,802 households that earn fewer than $25,000 a year (reported
from the 2008 Census). The median Canadian household is reported
to be $25,615 (2006 Canadian Census).

Some of you reading this might think that's not a big deal,
and it's just part of the way things are. Well, I see it differently. Let
me tell you why: if almost 25 percent of households in America
make fewer than $25,000, you might think that leaves room for
wealthy households. However the same statistics show that only 4.2
percent of American households earn $200,000 or more per year.
The winner is 21 million households earning somewhere between
$50,000–74,000 per year. This screamed one thing to me: it's time
to improve, and there is lots of room at the top!

I have spent years working with and interviewing millionaires
who started with very little and worked their way to the top. If they

can do it, you can do it. Whether you are in sales, working for a bank, the government or a union, if you have had enough and have been thinking about a change, reading those facts should make you want to take the second step today.

Why should you be willing to compromise what you are worth? I think you're worth more, and *you know* you're worth more!

Today, decide how much you are worth and what you have always dreamed of doing, and make yourself a promise that you are going to start working toward that. Be better than average!

The Unites States and Canada have almost 13 million self-employed people busy running their own business, 3.4 percent of people in the United States and 7.6 percent in Canada. Compare that 3.4 percent to the fact that only 4.2 percent of households earn more than $200,000 a year, and those numbers are pretty close. Also, 25 percent of the population 15 years and older is unemployed. That's 78 million people who have not yet found the spark inside them.

I have never been happy being a statistic of the average. For the past seven years, I strived to be above average, and the steps throughout the book show you how I went from the bottom 10 percent to the top 2 percent and didn't care to stop in the 88 percent in between, to where I wanted to be, where I felt I deserved to be, doing what I loved and earning what I felt I was worth.

Some of the wealthiest people I have ever had the opportunity to interview were people you wouldn't have known were at one time in the bottom 10 percent of those stats. They didn't have Hummers in the driveway or great big homes on the lake; they led simple lives, bought everything they could for cash and refused to owe anyone money for something they were going to enjoy. This is something that has intrigued me for years. On the flip side, I have met people who earn anywhere between $250,000–500,000 a year and have all the latest and greatest crazes of vehicles, high-end homes, fancy boats and big budgets. But they couldn't come up with $10,000 in cash if their lives depended on it. Is either way right or wrong? Who am I to say? However, it is my belief after living on both sides of the spectrum that you need to find your comfort zone. Decide if you want to be average or better than average!

Chapter 24

By-Products

*When people fear their government, there is tyranny. When
the government fears the people, there is liberty.*

—*Thomas Jefferson*

Governments thrive on people who are willing to accept life as it is
and not do what's best for them, who do not want to make their lives
better and start living their dreams. The governments thrive through
years of low median wage and high unemployment because the
control stays in the hands of the elected and appointed officials.

Can you imagine right now what it would be like if things were
the opposite of what they are? What if instead of 50 percent being in
the median and 10 percent being in the top, it was switched? What
do you think our world would be like if the numbers were more
even? Imagine if the statistics included more wealthy people in our
countries, if 65 or 70 percent of the population earned the majority
of the money. I will bet dollars to doughnuts that government would
change, schooling would change, people's attitudes would change,
the way recessions and depressions come and go would change and
life as we know it would change.

Don't get me wrong, this is just a thought to help you realize
that there are boundaries out there that are going to make it tough
for you to get to where you want to be, where you *need* to be.

There are four kinds of people in this world, and they are broken
into two different categories. In category one are the folks who know

they can change their lives and have everything they want, as well as the people who don't know it yet but are reading this and will soon know. In the other category are those who are going to try and keep others down at their miserable level, or try and prevent them from living the status quo; they are joined by the people who are going to try and pull others down once they start to see someone is on his way to living his dream.

If you ask someone on the street, he might tell you there are only two types, the rich and the poor. Those are people living in the second category—turn around and run when you meet them! Years ago a good friend said to me, "There are two types of salespeople in this world; there is Trev, and then there are those that want to be like Trev."

That was about the nicest thing this person had ever said to me. But he was onto something. He knew that I had spent years working toward having the privilege to be in the winner's circle. He also knew I had spent the last few years training and teaching others in my office. The point was clear that what mattered most was the separation. It didn't matter that I earned 10 times more or that they earned 10 times less, it isn't about money when it comes to those things. A sales profession is a perfect example that money is a by-product of doing something you love to do, and doing it well. When you do something that you're meant to do, and you do it with all your heart and soul, you will be rewarded with the by-product of doing an awesome job: money.

I have never in my career gone to work to earn money. That's like going to make money, and from previous chapters we know the only people who make money is the Mint. I go every morning to do something I love and to do it better than those people around me. If I had only put in half my heart and soul, I would have only been rewarded for half, and so forth. I do that one thing and make sure I do it to the best of my natural and trained abilities, and for it I am rewarded.

If you're willing to find your passion and put your heart and soul into it, you don't have to worry about the money being there, because it is a by-product and will be there when the time is right.

Chapter 25

Do You Want It Easy?

Pessimism is a very easy way out when you're considering what life really is, because pessimism is a short view of life—If you take a long view, I do not see how you can be pessimistic about the future of man or the future of the world.

—*Robertson Davies*

I am going to give you one simple yet absolute truth. You can have anything in life, live any kind of life you dream about, have as much money as you want or need and be anything ... as long as you follow the plan that is required to get you there. We need to lay out a plan for every action we take. Action comes from a decision of two choices.

When I was 19 years old, I had two decisions in front of me; one would prove to be the hardest decision, and one was without a doubt the simplest one. I could transfer with the company I was with and be an employee serving the clients of a multinational company, with my only reward being the satisfaction I gave myself, or I could choose a tougher path and start a business. I could choose a path that many people don't normally take, a path that causes sleepless nights, stress and a 65 percent failure rate. Based on that limited information, which path between those two choices would you take?

The easy choice was to stay with the big company, earn a pay cheque every two weeks, work from nine to five Monday through Friday and go home each night wondering what it would have been like if I had chosen the other path.

But you see, nothing ventured, nothing gained. If I failed in my decision to do something for myself, I would have failed trying and learned more from that than a lifetime of schooling. If I had failed, I would have been able to look and see why I failed, how I could change it if given the opportunity again and how I could succeed.

Well, the first time I did fail! But you know what? Failing at something that I knew I was to go after wasn't failing at all; it was learning with a C+ result. The choices we have in this life are based on what we are able to handle, how we can handle them and how they will better the lives of those around us.

A study was done recently on large lottery winners in North America. The results showed that one in three winners were broke and even in bankruptcy within five years of winning millions. These folks wanted to win the lottery so badly. In 1981, Lou Eisenberg won the largest lottery up to that date in the United States. He claimed his grand prize of $5,000,000 at the age of 53. He was an instant household name. Everyone wanted to be him, meet him and live that dream of going from earning $225 a week changing light bulbs to becoming an instant multi-millionaire. Let's fast forward almost thirty years, to today. He is 81 years old. The story *should* read that he spent a posh retirement living off the interest the money has earned over the years, and he is celebrating his wealth now on his third decade. It doesn't. The story finishes with the fact that he now earns $250 per week and lives in a mobile home in Florida after spending millions on holidays, personal problems and lavish (yet wrong) spending choices.

These stories are heard everywhere, and the reason I share them with you is that, yes, it would be great to win the lottery not having to work to earn millions of dollars, and money just falling in your lap sounds like a dream. But it is just that, a dream. If you want to be a millionaire, we have gone over different ways to become one: save to be one, work to be one, earn to be one. Just don't sit there and dream about being one, or you might as well just keep buying lottery tickets for a full-time career instead of stepping your life up and taking control today.

On the flip side of the story of the lottery winner, how many times do you hear about folks earning their way to the multi-millionaire status? There are just under 9 million millionaires in the world today. A little less than 3 million of those millionaires are in North America. So one-third of the world's millionaires are in the United States, Canada, and Mexico. In the coming years, there is a real possibility that 168,000 new millionaires will be added to that list. That's what blows my mind!

So let's imagine the scenarios together. One thousand multi-million-dollar lottery winners will be added to the list of multi-millionaires at the same time that 167,000 income earners are going to be added. The best part yet is that five years from now, 90 percent of the income earners will still be on that growing list, but only two-thirds of the lottery winners will be.

I mentioned I was at a fork in the road and had to make a choice. I made the tough choice, I made the choice to go out on my own, not work for someone who was going to tell me what I was worth or what I was going to make. I wasn't going to buy a lottery ticket every week in hopes I would be the next big winner. I was going to start a life that I could see in my mind and become everything I had ever wanted to be. No, it wasn't even close to being easy. Yes, I struggled for a year or two, but what did I have to lose besides losing?

I am trying to drive this point home: when you work for it, when it is your mental planning day in and day out, or your blood, sweat and tears that go into making you and your company what it is, that's when you know you have done it. You have done something that only a small percent of people manage to do.

The best and easiest part is it is being done every day, so that means it is more than achievable for you, your sister, your neighbour, your friend or your coworker. The question then becomes, who is going to be added to that list next? You are!

While building my career and starting to shape the life I had seen for myself, I had one saying that I did not waiver from. No matter the market conditions, the season or the mood I was in, I never stopped believing that I could do it, and I never once let this saying that I wrote out of my sight.

Live your life for tomorrow, not yesterday, and just spend today enjoying it to the fullest!

Chapter 26

You're a Winner!

The experienced mountain climber is not intimidated by a mountain—
he is inspired by it. The persistent winner is not discouraged by a
problem—he is challenged by it. Mountains are created to be conquered;
adversities are designed to be defeated. Problems are sent to be solved.
It is better to master one mountain than a thousand foothills.

—*William Arthur Ward*

Welcome to the winner's chapter! This chapter is dedicated to helping you view yourself and everything you do as a winner. Have you ever met someone at a meeting and left thinking, "Wow, are they cocky, self-confident and arrogant?" Arrogance is the exact opposite of confidence, and 95 percent of the time, a very insecure person lies just below the surface. Cocky is generally someone who is young and has done very well for himself because something was in their favour (i.e., the market, the season, etc.). Self-confidence (which is my favourite term) is someone who has been welcomed into the winner's circle and has learned the power that comes with this self-image.

When you start to think like a winner, the have nots, have dos and boo-hoos don't matter to your way of thinking anymore. They are still there—because trust me, they will never leave—but you don't let them affect your thinking. Life changes when you change. When you decide that it is time to take charge and change your life, great doors of opportunity start to open for you.

In the past decade I have had amazing opportunities present themselves to me because I was in the right mind-set to not only notice them but accept them and make the best I possibly could out of them. I was in the winner's circle, and my attitude changed about everything I did in my life. It was then that I knew I truly had become the best in my field.

Don't get me wrong, there were others in my field that made as much money or even more money than me, and it's great that those 10 percent join me in the circle. But the other 90 percent had no idea what the circle was, and they may still not know.

Here is the breakdown. When you get so good at what you do that you're confident in your decisions, you're willing to learn about what it is you do and you take unbelievable pride in everything you work so hard toward, you are invited into this circle without even knowing it. All you know is that people start to treat you a little better, because they can tell. It's sort of like the concept that a dog can smell fear. Well, people can sense confidence, and it's not only the way you dress or the way you look. It's in what you give off. But beware—people can also sense arrogance, and trust me, that is one scent you don't want to have lingering around you!

Some of the people you see on TV right now will go either of those ways. Oprah Winfrey might as well be the president of the winner's circle! When you can do the amazing things for the world that this woman has done and be able to give back to the people who helped her get to where she is, that's winner's class! Yet on the flip side you see actors, singers or different TV personalities acting up, being rude and living an arrogant life; they are the lottery winners of the real world. They hit it big in one or two events and let the success, fame and money go straight to the wrong place. One out of three invariably disappears off the scene and has financial trouble.

Take this chapter how you will; I am hoping you take it as a warning. You want to get to the winner's circle by doing it honestly and wholesomely. You want to earn your way to the top with style and class. You want to find someone you know who may have the winning attitude and ask her to share with you how she arrived at it. And the best thing about someone in the winner's circle is that she wants to share it with those that deserve it. So show people you deserve it and come and join them at the top!

Chapter 27

Think it, Believe it, See it!

Believe it can be done. When you believe something can be done, really believe, your mind will find the ways to do it. Believing a solution paves the way to solution.

—*David Joseph Schwartz*

Have you ever heard or read about someone speaking of or thinking his or her way to riches? You probably thought, "Yeah right, easy for them to say! They're the one with the riches!" What if I told you it was true? People are doing it every day and don't even know it. We have discussed at length throughout this book how your thinking affects your life. When you think positively, act positively and offer positive actions to those around you, positive things start to come to you. That's simple, and by now you should be well on your way to changing your thinking. However, once you change to positive thinking, you need to set it up to think about the right sort of things.

Take me for example. From the time I started selling real estate, I wanted to own multiple real estate companies. It was much more than a goal or a dream or even a passion. It was what I saw in store for my life. One of my good friends and esteemed colleagues also wanted to own a real estate company. Today, I own a company and he does not, and that's for one simple reason: we thought about it differently. I thought about it every day. I put in the work that was required, performed my tasks with an attribute in the office of a realtor and saw one thing in my mind's eye: the owner at the time coming to me and offering me the opportunity to buy the office. My good friend always *assumed* he would own the office. He *saw* himself owning it in his mind, I am quite sure, however he failed to put together the missing link, which was *how* he was going to own it.

You don't have to have every detail spelled out in colour when you are thinking your way to riches, but you need a majority of them readily available in your mind's eye. I thought myself right into owning multiple real estate offices with my partners, whom I cherish, and they, both the offices and my partners, were a part of my mind's eye plan of thinking my way to riches.

Everything we do in today's world requires structure—our budgets, our bills, our housing, our taxes—so why shouldn't the same apply to our dreams, hopes and goals? You cannot do your household budget just by saying, "I will pay my mortgage, my car payment and my insurance this month and be good to go." You need to put structure and detail into your life, stand back and watch the results start to change.

Start thinking your way to riches today. At the beginning of the book, you wrote down your goals and what it would mean to you to accomplish them. We decided a timeline on how you could achieve them. Now is the time to start putting them into action! Review those goals every day, and when you review them, you are going to see the plan in your mind's eye. As you go throughout your day, there is going to be certain things that remind you of your goals, and that is going to trigger you to think about the ways that you are accomplishing them and how much they mean to you. And your life has already started to change for the better.

I am a doodler. My wife gives me a hard time about it, my mother always did and my staff is constantly throwing out work documents and redoing them because I doodle on them. If you were to take a collection of doodlers and put 15 of us in a room together, chances are all of us would doodle something different. Next time you're doodling, or if you were on the phone today and did, have a look and see what you doodled most. You see, doodling is how our mind reflects what is going on in it most of the time.

I constantly doodle three or four different objects: the first one is a star, the second one is dollar signs, the third one is the "at" symbol and the fourth one is a home. When I go through the list and look at what each of them means to me, they all tie into one another. The star I doodle for belief, passion, strength, faith and desire. The dollar signs do not just represent money; they represent freedom, independence, security and the life my family and I live. The third and fourth symbols are usually together "@ home." These mean my family, my time, peace in my mind and disruption from everyday stresses.

I have programmed my mind to think about the things that matter to me the most all the time, whether I am aware of it or not. When I talk in my sleep, I talk about the things I love to do, the people with which I love to spend time. My wife lies in bed at night and wonders if she should answer me or just try to block me out. My mind is working whether I know it or not, and it is programmed to bring me what I desire the most in life.

This will come to you as you start to take charge and change your life. I am not saying you are going to be an instant doodler artist or anything of the sort. Once you program your mind to work with you on your desires, you will be amazed how quickly they come to you.

So, let me ask you, "What do you desire?"

Chapter 28

If You Won't, Who Will?

When it comes to getting things done, we need
fewer architects and more bricklayers.

—*Colleen C. Barrett*

No one is responsible for you. Take me for example, helping you get everything out of life that you desire and are willing to work toward. I am not responsible *for* you, to make sure you do what I tell you to do, to make sure your goals are done and that you read them twice a day. I am, however, responsible *to* you. I am responsible to make sure that I can help you hit the goals that *you* have placed out—but *you* are responsible *for you*. The next time something goes awry or turns upside down, instead of blaming it on someone else or making excuses as to why it didn't get done, just own it. Say to yourself, "I am responsible." This is one of the most liberating statements you can ever make, and it frees you from everything else you were about to do—excuses, fibs, blame.

I use that statement all the time. We are human and make mistakes. We are allowed to make mistakes, because that's how we learn. All that matters at the end of the day is that we fix the mistakes we made and we learn from them. If we were not supposed to make mistakes, we would have a manual from birth detailing every day and year of our lives. But we don't, so we have to make mistakes, get our feelings hurt as a child, have our hearts broken as a teen, maybe experience a business failure or a loss of savings, and everything and anything else that life offers so that we learn that we are responsible, that only we can take charge of our own lives and change them.

Today is the day you give up being the manager of the universe. Truly, I have just resigned you from that position; you weren't getting paid enough anyways. You don't care what others think of Sally in accounting; that's their problem to deal with. You don't care what Peter in HR thinks about the way you do your job because you do a damn good job, and yes, you may have only given 75 percent today, but tomorrow you are going to give 100 percent. That's all that matters to you!

You are all that matters to you. Your goals, you dreams, your plans and your life are your top priority for you, from this day forward. You will no longer let someone else dictate what you get or what you deserve. You will not let the evening news control how you live your life or go after what you deserve. From this day forward, everything you do is for you and your family!

Chapter 29

If I Had a Million Dollars ...

Being rich is having money; being wealthy is having time.

—*Margaret Bonnano*

Back in the mid 1990s, the Bare Naked Ladies came out with a song of what they would do if they had $1,000,000. If you had $1,000,000, what would you do? Ask yourself right now and just go with what the answer is. The first answer is going to be your true desire.

When I first asked myself this question, I thought I would slow down with sales and start writing and helping people to be their best. The theory behind this question is that if you could do anything you wanted to do and not have to worry about money every day, that's what you *should be doing* today. By doing what you love each day, in and out, you will never work a day in your life. This is the right we hold; we are born with it, but somewhere along the way, people lose hold of it. Well, if you have lost it, this is you grabbing back what is rightfully yours—the right to happiness.

If you follow your heart and be true to yourself, you will come out on top. Sometimes it won't seem like it is there; sometimes it will feel like you are just trying to grasp at air. But trust me, bobbing for air on top is a long way from beating your way off the bottom, and it is only a short distance to swimming to shore.

Look at the people you know or have heard of that have a million dollars and ask yourself if they are doing something they truly love.

I have met a lot of millionaires in my life, and I wonder if they love life and are doing what they always wanted to. The answer is usually yes. Of course there are the ones that get to that status and don't know how to control it or handle it, but that's a whole other book in itself.

Everything goes back to what we discussed about by-products, earning a living and doing what you do well. If you can live in harmony and be true to yourself, you will have $1,000,000, and by following the steps in this guide to life, it will grow without you even knowing. Like attracts like, money attracts money and happiness is the very same—these are tangible items you deserve in your life today, and it's about time you have an abundance of them.

Right now, just focus on your dreams and goals, and strive toward what you would do every day if you had a million dollars sitting in your bank account. The first step to taking charge and changing your life is the ability to see not only where you are today, but what you will be doing tomorrow. Plan it with absolute faith and live the dream you deserve!

Chapter 30

It's Only the Beginning!

There are two mistakes one can make along the road to truth... not going all the way, and not starting.

—*Buddha*

By now, you have your goals all laid out for the next 10 to 20 years. You can add to them, modify them, move them up and move them around, but the most important part is done. They are written out and easily accessible for you to cross reference, check off and review on a daily basis.

You have come to realize that having the right attitude toward life will ultimately control the results you are achieving. How you think will affect your life on the outside, including all things around you.

You should be able to see the things in life you want to change and should now be picturing them changed with your mind's eye every night before bed and every morning after you finish saying your gratuities.

You should now be saving something from every pay cheque in a separate account or having your employer do it for you. Whether it is 5, 10 or 15 percent, the amount doesn't matter right now. What matters is that you are following through on a promise that you made to yourself.

You are seeking the help of others to get you through these times. If it is money management you're having difficulties with, or time management, or even just assistance in getting your mind and body in harmony, there are people who specialize in helping others with these things.

Humans have great potential to do one thing extremely well, whether that be a certain sport, work with metals, work with people, sales or more. Everything else they decide to do at the same time is a secondary enjoyment and will usually only be done at 80 percent. So do what you know how to do extremely well and seek the help of others for that which you do not.

I am extremely excited that we have journeyed this far together to Take Charge and Change Your Life Today. As I have mentioned many times, I am responsible to you but not for you. Check out my website at www.bolininternational.com and register under the Take Charge and Change Your Life Today tab. There is an amazing amount of useful information there free for you, to help you become the very best you can be.

Thank you for having the desire to change, and congratulations on taking the first step. Today is the day you take charge and change your life. You deserve it!

About the Author

Born and raised in Fort St. John, British Columbia, Canada, Trevor Bolin entered the business world of real estate at the age of 20. Whether as a realtor, owner of several real estate companies, inspirational speaker or sales coach, Trevor still loves to help people accomplish their dreams. He resides in and maintains his businesses in Fort St. John, British Columbia, with his beautiful wife and two sons.

Trevor is currently working on his next books, *The Secret to Sales* and *Silent Tears,* his autobiography.